Racey Recipes

Sylvia Davis, Loti Irwin, Jean Johnson
Anne Kimpton, Cate Russell, Georgie Shaw

Profits from this book will go to UNICEF

First published 1999 by The Racey Recipe Group
(in association with Debowe Publishing)
Weavers, Fewcott, Bicester, Oxfordshire OX6 9NZ

ISBN 1-902081-05-6

The recipe for Grilled Langoustines appears by kind permission of Ruth Rogers
and Rose Gray of the River Café.
David Coulthard's recipe for Mince and Tatties and Pit Stop Soufflé appears by
kind permission of Bazal Productions.

To the best of our knowledge all recipies in this book are the personal recipies of
the celebrities that gave them to us. In the event of the recipe not being the
celebrities own, the recipe given is the creation of one of the Racey Recipe Group
or their friends.

A copy of this book is available from the British Library.

Cover design by Andy Morton
Page design by Joel Francis
Printed by The Works, Newbury
HBS Design Associates
Suite One, Phoenix Brewery, Bartholomew Street
Newbury, Berkshire RG14 5QA

FORWARD
BY JOHN SURTEES M.B.E.

Motor sport has given most of the contributors to this book the opportunity to see the world and taste it's gastronomic delights.

It's also given them a fair taste of the basics of life - sheltering from the cold in draughty garages, local speciality snacks in cafés and hostelries at the end of late-night car preparation sessions and makeshift meals in car transporters.

Here they share with you their favourite recipes... everything from apple crumble to chicken vindaloo, with lashings of bucatini and tonkatsu thrown in for good measure.

Whether they have taken full advantage of all the opportunities their travels afforded them is for you to judge. This book – which contains everything from mum's home cooking to cuisine at it's finest – will provide some of the answers.

One thing it certainly highlights is all that's modern isn't necessarily best. Take the modern Grand Prix drivers with their built to fit Grand Prix cars, personal fitness gurus and carefully tuned diets... these dishes would not look out of place in a coronary care unit. No way (and no need) for them to remove that extra padding in the seat to facilitate entry and exit. So perhaps we of an earlier generation had some advantages. We were able to enjoy the best of mum's cooking at home and the best of the rest of the world... and still squeeze into the cockpit!

So – like me – scan these pages and pick the recipes that take your fancy, taking comfort from the fact that you're helping one of the worthiest causes around. You'll be in good company.

Bon appetito!

ACKNOWLEDGEMENTS

We would like to thank the contributors and the following for all their help, advise, encouragement, sponsorship and general support while we were putting together Racey Recipes:

Translators:
Francoise Austin (French),
Baerbel Clarke, Baerbel Vosgroene (German),
Padraic Healey (Italian), Andrew Wilkinson (Japanese),
Virginia Cardoso (Portuguese)

Bernie Ecclestone, AP Racing, BRDC, Castle Combe Circuit,
Castrol, Demon Tweeks, Duke Marketing, Corporate Jets,
International Motorsports Hall of Fame, Mallory Park, Maranello Sales,
Mobil, M.W.S., Page & Moy, Rockingham Raceway

Evesham Micros, Mono Equipment

John Blunsden, Maurice Hamilton, Jonathan Legard,
Joe Saward, Simon Taylor

Jim Bamber, Don Grant

Andrew Eborn
Howden Ganley at the British Racing Drivers' Club
Tony Schulp

Louise O'Gorman
PhotOiG Studios, Display & Advertising Photography, Woodlands,
Molewood, Hertford, Herts SG14 2PL
Dan R. Boyd
David Hayhoe
43 New Barn Lane, Uckfield, East Sussex TN22 5EL
Motorsport Images
The Chapel, 61 Watling Street, Towcester, Northants NN12 6AG
Margaret Money

For the photographs from
Lynton Money
Crispin Thruston
Sporting Pictures (UK) Ltd.,
7a Lambs Conduit Passage, Holborn, London WC1R 4RG

Mark Smith, Tim Christian, Andy Morton, Joel Francis, Lee Stevens

Piers Johnson, Simone Grant

Gil Adshead, Robin and Trisha Bradford, Primmie Bright,
Hazel Carter, Howden and Judy Ganley, Jonathan Gill, Alison Hill,
Snow Irwin, Alexander Irwin, Gwyneth Lyddon, Scarlet Couriers,
Mauro Serra, Rupert Sheldon, Giselle Sohm,
John and Jane Surtees, Elizabeth Watt, Derek Wright

Michelle Dempster, Parchment Printers, Bicester, Oxfordshire
Bookspeed, Coys Archives, Grand Prix TopGear,
Denys Rohan, Silverstone Circuits Ltd

All team and drivers' Press Officers and Managers for their invaluable
assistance and co-operation and to everyone who has helped and will be
helping to promote and publicise Racey Recipes.

During the compilation of Racey Recipes, several publications were
referred to of which the most useful were:
Magazines – Autosport, F1 News, F1 Racing. The Complete Encyclopaedia
of Formula One, Jones. Grand Prix Data Book 1997, Hayhoe & Holland.
Grand Prix Guide 1950-1998, Deschenaux. IndyCar Racing Handbook 1972,
Phillips. Motorsport Yearbook 1972, Gill. Who Works in Formula One,
Gregoire. Who Works in Indy Cars, Gregoire.

FORWARD
BY JACKIE STEWART O.B.E.

"Being part of the motor racing fraternity, either as a driver, a co-team owner or one of the many other avenues involved in motor racing, food is always a very important part of that life. It can be eating in glamorous restaurants in exotic locations, or eating in very poor restaurants in terrible places, and other times it is being at home with your wife enjoying your own food as a family. In my particular case, as time has gone by, the latter gives me the greatest pleasure and the least indigestion.

Helen, thankfully, is a wonderful cook. Sadly I am not of the generation that allowed men to be in any way skilled in the kitchen. If it were left to me it would be beans on toast which, incidentally, I adore. The many recipes that appear in this wonderful book represent a galaxy of talent unmatched in the motor racing world and gives you, the reader the opportunity to recognise that there are a great many dishes that suit the pallet of a great variety of people who enjoy the culinary arts of others.

The list of the chosen dishes sometimes are very clearly obvious when Gerhard Berger chooses Wiener Schnitzel or David Coulthard chooses Mince and Tatties and it is not at all surprising that Mario Andretti would choose Gnocchi coming originally from Italy.

Whatever the choices that you may take from this extravaganza of flavours,
I am sure it will be a very useful Bible in the kitchen for titillating the taste buds
and certainly allowing for elements of change coming into what might otherwise
be a boring life of a stable diet."

Yours sincerely

[signature: Jackie Stewart]

INDEX

Eddie and Marie Jordan	Warm Irish Potato and Black Pudding
Mike and Anne Kimpton	Ginger and Orange Marinated Lamb
Pedro Lamy	Spaghetti Carbonara
Doreen Leston	Chilli Con Carné
Charles Lucas	Karlskoga Trout
Klaus Ludwig	Wild Boar
Nigel Mansell	Pork Fillet in Port
Nick Mason	Goat's Cheese Salad, Spinach and Goat's Cheese Tart, Bouillabaisse, Rouille
Pat McLaren Brickett	Pavlova
Allan McNish	Haggis
Alain Menu	Pave au Chocolate
Gian Carlo Minardi	Tagliatelli
Alan Minshaw	Caesar Salad
Lord and Lady Montagu	Drop Dead Delicious Cake
Max Mosley	Grilled Langoustines
Stirling and Susie Moss	Salmon Mousse
Shinji Nakano	Tonkatsu
Don and Joanne Naman	Coconut Cake, Cream Cheese Brownies, Chicken Pot Pie, Chocolate Caramel Pecan Cheesecake, Red Velvet Cake
Tiff Needell	Lobster Thermidor
Count and Countess Ouvaroff	Pork and Apricots (Sally Barking Mad)
Olivier Panis	Poached Salmon
Richard Petty	Stuffed Green Peppers, Angel Food Cake
Craig Pollock	Mince and Tatties
Harvey Postlethwaite	Tigella
Alain Prost	Minestrone, Chicken Basquaise
Paul Radisich	Pavlova
Bobby Rahal	Scallop Ravioli
Ricardo Rosset	Bucatini with Meat and Red Pepper Sauce
Mika Salo	Spaghetti Carbonara
Michael and Corinna Schumacher	Knuckle of Veal, Dumplings and Red Cabbage
Ralf Schumacher	Spicy Penne Pasta
Georgie Shaw	Lethal Chocolate, Thingy. Paris-Brest
Giselle Sohm	Tomato and Basil Sauce
Jackie and Helen Stewart	Fettuccini
Paul and Victoria Stewart	Chocolate Pecan Pie
Danny Sullivan	Veal Piccata
John and Jane Surtees	Crab Claws and Prawns in Red Curry
John Thornburn	Warm Salmon Salad, Tarte au Citron, Prune and Apple Cake, Armagnac Ice Cream, Breast of Wood Pigeon, Cotswold Trout, Chinese Soup
Jean Todt	Pasta with Olive Oil and Parmesan, Escalope Milanaise
Jarno Trulli	Squid with Tomato Sauce, Pizza Blanca
Ken Tyrrell	Veal Casserole
Al Unser	Strawberry Dip
Al Unser Jnr.	Victory Lane Quesadillas
Jacques Villeneuve	Sugar Pie
Joe Waldron	Escalopes of Veal 'Brownie'
Murray Walker	Chicken Vindaloo
Prof. Sid Watkins	Nigerian Curry
John Watson	Lobster
Sir Frank Williams	Soup á la Ginny Williams
Alessandro Zanardi	Pasta with Broccoli

To all our friends past and present,

To the perfect lap and to lapping back markers,

To the dream machine and the start money special,

To soaking up the sun in Monaco and to soaking wet in Silverstone,

To your very own paddock pass and having to pay to watch a club race,

To all night parties and all night engine rebuilds,

To haute cuisine in the paddock and tepid tea in the circuit canteen,

To your first podium and your last chance,

To the excitement, the hype, the hope, the anticipation and

To shattered dreams, the exhaustion, the despair, the frustration,

To next weekend . . .

To motor racing.

There are moments when the best ideas simply refuse to work and then others that simply take off, generating a momentum all their own. Racey Recipes, despite the occasional setback is definitely one of the latter. From the start we have been constantly surprised, delighted and very grateful for all the help and support we have received.

For a sport which has a reputation for being, shall we say, gastronomically challenged, the recipes show just how many drivers are really closet gourmets! We seemed to have tapped into a mine of culinary gold and since all the profits from the book are going to UNICEF, we certainly hope so.

So taste, enjoy and eat like a racer.

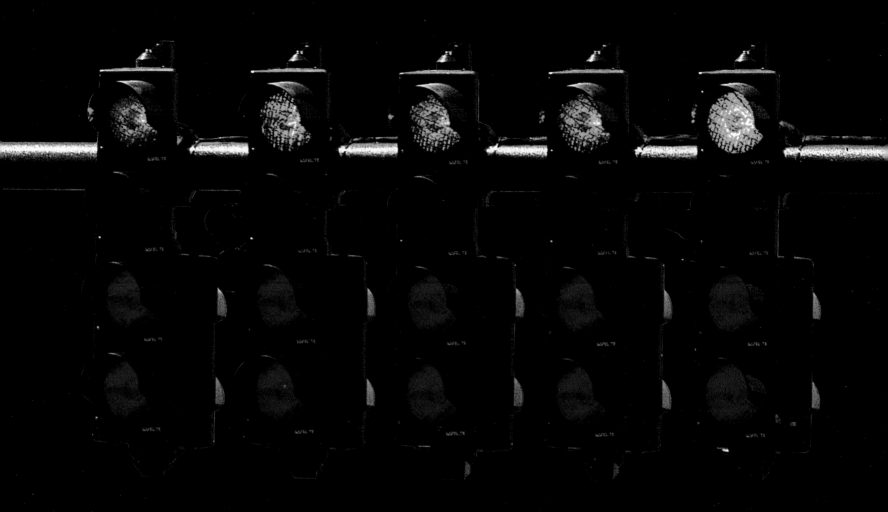

starters

Bearne/Sutton

STIRLING AND SUSIE MOSS

TUNA OR SALMON MOUSSE

1 can condensed tomato soup
1 packet (8oz/240g) of cream cheese
1 cup diced green pepper
1 cup diced celery
1 small grated onion
1 cup mayonnaise
1 large can tuna or salmon (remove skin and bones)
2 tblsp unflavoured gelatine
1/2 cup cold water

Having watched it being done, I can promise you that this is incredibly easy to make. So much so that I could even do it myself - if pushed. Very fortunately, I have not yet been that pushed!

For picnics and snack eating, the mousse doesn't need to be turned out. Just leave it in a suitable bowl and let people scoop it out with a spoon or treat it like a dip and dig into it with crackers, crisps, raw vegetables etc. When it comes to more formal occasions, Susie quite often turns it out of a ring mould onto a big plate filling the middle with a devilled tomato salad and surrounding the whole thing with Mediterranean prawns, lemon wedges and mixed leaves.

Good luck with the book and much love to Sylvia. Ciao, Stirling.

Melt in a double boiler the tomato soup and cream cheese. When cooled, put in green pepper, diced celery, mayonnaise and fish. For a smoother mousse, combine cooled mixture with mayonnaise and fish in a blender or food processor before adding vegetables.

Then add gelatine which has been dissolved in the cold water. Pour into oiled fish or other mould and chill until set.

Stirling Moss OBE
1952 2nd Monte Carlo Rally
2nd in Formula 1 World Championship 1955, 1956, 1957, 1958
1955 won the Mille Miglia with Denis Jenkinson, Mercedes 300 SLR
Won the Targa Florio with Peter Collins for Mercedes
1950 Formula 2 Driver: HWM
1951-1972 Formula 1 Driver: ERA, Connaught, Cooper, Maserati, Mercedes, Vanwall, Lotus

One of the greatest racing legends who became a household name in the fifties (And the police's standard line when apprehending speeding motorists: "Who d'you think you are. Stirling Moss?"). Moss was the first British driver to win the British Grand Prix in a British car (Aintree in 1957 with Vanwall); he also gave Lotus their first Grand Prix win (Monaco 1960) for Rob Walker. Stirling's famous 1955 Mille Miglia win with Jenks, at an average speed approaching 98mph (record) stands as testament to his exceptional driving skills. An active Patron of the Goodwood Festival of Speed and Goodwood Motor Circuit, Stirling still enjoys his racing and makes several guest appearances at historic events throughout the world.

BARBA GIUAN (OR RISSOLES)

Sporting Pictures (UK)

Make short pastry with the flour, margarine or butter, salt and water.

Place in bowl, cover and place in refrigerator until needed.

Mince and boil the Swiss chards.

Brown a minced onion in a saucepan and mix with the boiled Swiss chard, one egg, Parmesan cheese, salt and pepper.

Roll the pastry into a thin sheet which you cut into round pieces, (the size of a glass will do).

On the half of each round put a teaspoon of the mixture.

Fold the pastry as in an apple turn-over and seal with egg yolk.

Fry the rissoles in oil, and serve hot with tomato sauce.

FOR SHORT PASTRY
250g (8½ oz) flour
100g (3½ oz) margarine or butter
salt
water

FILLING
swiss chards
1 onion, minced
1 egg
freshly grated parmesan cheese
salt and pepper
oil for frying

Kinrade/Sutton

RICHARD AND LYNDA PETTY

STUFFED GREEN PEPPERS

Legendary driver of NASCAR car #43
NASCAR Winston Cup all time Career Wins Leader (200)
7 time Winston Cup Champion
7 time Daytona 500 winner
Received U.S. Medal of Freedom 1992

1 ½ lbs ground beef
1 medium onion, chopped fine
1 tblsp chilli powder
2 eggs
1 cup of catsup
1 cup cornflakes
salt and pepper to taste
6 bell peppers cut in half and cleaned

SAUCE
2 ½ cups of catsup and tomato paste,
(use more catsup than paste)
2 tblsp brown sugar
2 tblsp ground mustard
1 tblsp vinegar

Boil the peppers for 5 minutes.

Mix all the other ingredients together.

Stuff peppers with the mixture and arrange in the bottom of a large Pyrex dish.

Mix sauce together, pour over peppers.

Bake at 375F/190C/Gas mark 5 for 30 to 40 minutes.

Kinrade/Sutton

Rockingham
Britain's motorsports complex for the new millennium

9 times Winner Formula 1 World Constructors' Championship
1980, 1981, 1986, 1987, 1992, 1993, 1994, 1996, 1997
7 times Winner Formula 1 World Drivers' Chamionship
1980, 1982, 1987, 1992, 1993, 1996, 1997

SIR FRANK WILLIAMS

SOUPE A LA GINNY WILLIAMS

Founder and Team Principal of Williams Grand Prix Engineering
1968 Founded Williams, 1972 Entered the Formula 1 World Championship

Sutton

Frank Williams started his successful racing career as a driver, before moving into team management. WilliamsF1 has been one of the most successful Grand Prix teams in the history of Formula 1 racing. Frank Williams and his team's extraordinary successes were recognised in the 1999 New Year's Honours List when Frank Williams received a Knighthood.

Ginny brought this recipe back from the South of France a few years ago, adapted, I am informed from Soupe ou Pistou. We do not like garlic so that is left out but it can be included in great quantities if liked. It is delicious, very thick and we eat it every Sunday evening when I am not at a Grand Prix.

In the largest pan you can find, heat a few tablespoons of olive oil.

Start roughly chopping the vegetables in the list order and add to the pan, allowing the onions to brown a little before adding all the rest.

Allow them to sweat for ten minutes before throwing in the basil and a large glug of olive oil.

The soup benefits from lots of oil and basil.

Cover with chicken stock, pop the lid on the pan and place in a medium oven or the bottom right hand oven in a four oven Aga for at least three hours.

Blast it with a hand held food processor or put in the blender, it should be left quite coarse.

Season with salt and pepper.

A few basil leaves pounded with some olive oil drizzled on top is nice.

very good olive oil
1 chopped onion
2 large potatoes
1 medium leek
a few celery branches
5 large carrots
2 large courgettes
3 handfuls of fine green beans
6 tomatoes
1 tin red kidney beans, drained
1 tin cannelini beans, drained
a generous bunch of basil
a couple of pints of fresh chicken stock

Titan Group

PAULINE HAILWOOD

SALADE DE FOIE GRAS CHAUDE

Wife of the late Mike Hailwood, Nine-times Motor-cycle World Champion, Twelve-times winner IoM TT, won Senior IoM TT again in 1979
Formula 1 Driver: Reg Parnell Racing, Surtees, McLaren

I love cooking and trying out new recipes, I am sending you 5 recipes of dishes that I have prepared many times, never have had a problem with and always go down well, I do hope you like them.

350g (12oz) mixed salad leaves
i.e. watercress, curly endive,
radicchio, oakleaf lettuce
30ml (2 tblsp) chopped fresh herbs,
chives, parsley, tarragon, basil etc
100g (4oz) french beans, trimmed
and blanched for 2 minutes
2 firm tomatoes, skinned,
de-seeded and cut into 8
or 12 cherry tomatoes (easier)
15g (¹/₂oz) butter
15ml (1 tblsp) olive oil
1 small red onion, cut into rings
50g (2oz) button mushrooms, sliced
100g (4oz) pate de foie gras
aux truffles, cut into 12 slices
or chicken livers cut into bite size
pieces and sauteed in a little butter
until just slightly pink on the inside.

DRESSING
45ml (3 tblsp) olive or walnut oil
30ml (2 tblsp) raspberry vinegar
5 ml (1 tsp) green peppercorns
5ml (1 tsp) Dijon or Meaux mustard
5ml (1 tsp) sugar
salt and pepper

Wash all salad leaves and tear into bite sized pieces, place in a large bowl with the herbs, beans and tomatoes.

Melt the butter with the oil in a frying pan and fry the onion rings until golden.

Add the mushrooms and toss quickly in the fat.

Keep warm. If using chicken livers, in a separate pan, melt a little butter and fry as described above. Keep warm after removing from pan.

Put all the dressing ingredients into a pan and whisk over a gentle heat until warmed through.

Season generously.

Add to the salad and toss quickly, coating the leaves evenly with the dressing.

Place at once onto individual serving plates and top with slices of pâté de foie gras or the chicken livers.

Serve immediately whilst still warm and do not mix the warm dressing with the leaves too early or the leaves will go limp.

LAYERED SALAD

I don't have the quantities for this recipe, as it was just shown to me by an American friend. Normally, I just make up as much as I think I need plus a bit more, because it keeps for several days and is great in sandwiches.

crispy lettuce such as iceberg, celery, spring onions, frozen peas, mayonnaise, cheese (hard, Cheddar or Parmesan), crispy bacon

In a glass straight sided serving dish; place a layer of crisp lettuce leaves such as iceberg, torn or chopped into bite sized pieces. Then chop or slice some celery and sprinkle over the lettuce in a thinnish layer.

Trim and wash some spring onions, finely chop and make another layer over the lettuce and celery.

Cook some frozen peas, adding a spoonful of sugar to the pan, strain, refresh and when cool make this the next layer (Cook enough to give a good covering.).

Follow this with a layer of mayonnaise, (Hellmans) again making a good covering.

Top this with grated cheese, I normally use Cheddar, and for the final layer, grill some bacon until really crisp, allow to cool on some kitchen paper to absorb the fat. When cool, break into small pieces and sprinkle over the cheese.

Serve like this, but when dishing out, try to get all the layers per serving and guests can combine them with the mayonnaise on their plate, or you can mix it a little as you serve it.

The salad will keep longer if you don't toss the whole thing and just leave it in layers.

Chris Meek sponsors Pauline Hailwood's Racey Recipe

4 times Formula One World Champion 1985, 1986, 1989, 1993
1980-1993 Formula 1 Driver: McLaren, Renault, Ferrari, Williams
Grand Prix wins: 51
Owner of Prost Grand Prix

ALAIN PROST

ITALIAN MINESTRONE

Team Principal Prost Grand Prix
Owner of Prost Grand Prix

Prost GP

*Since hanging up his helmet and closing the record
books on his hugely successful racing career, Alain
was appointed as special Ambassador to the Renault
Group until 1995, he moved to McLaren as Special
Consultant and Adviser before purchasing the former
Ligier Formula 1 team in 1997 (renamed, Prost
Grand Prix). 1998 Prost Grand Prix relocated from
Magny-Cours to a new purpose built facility outside
Paris. Alain retains his two drivers for the 1999
season - Olivier Panis and Jarno Trulli.*

*Alain was introduced to Italian Minestrone by Luigi Montanini
who was the Ferrari chef when Alain was racing for them.
It's still one of his favourites as Luigi now cooks for
Prost Grand Prix. An ideal hearty and healthy meal
for a cold night at the circuit.*

This is not Luigi's recipe but one of our favourites.

Heat the oil in a large pan.

Add the pork, garlic, onion, parsley, oregano and pepper.

Cook for about 10 minutes until ingredients begin to brown.

Add the tomato purée and half a cup of the stock.

Cook for another 5 minutes.

Add all the vegetables, the beans and the remaining stock.

Simmer for 45 minutes.

Add the noodles and cook for a further 10 minutes.

Serve in a large tureen sprinkled with the Parmesan cheese.

8oz (225g) salt belly of pork,
skinned and diced
1 garlic clove, finely chopped
1 onion, chopped
1 tsp (5ml) chopped fresh parsley
1 tsp (5ml) chopped fresh oregano
1 tsp (5ml) olive oil
$\frac{1}{2}$ tsp (2.5ml) freshly ground
 black pepper
1 tblsp (15ml) tomato purée
2 pints (1.2 litres) vegetable or
chicken stock
2 carrots, diced
3 sticks of celery, chopped
2 potatoes, diced
8oz (225g) cooked haricot beans
4 oz (100g) fresh or frozen peas
4 tomatoes, peeled and chopped
4 oz (100g) fine noodles
2 tsp (30ml) fresh grated
Parmesan cheese

PhotO'G

6

SQD LDR ANDY GREEN OBE

CHILLI PICKLE

Driver of THRUST SSC
Holder of the World Land Speed Record at 763mph

1 bunch of fresh coriander
1 bunch of fresh mint
6 or 7 green chillies
1 tsp chilli powder
$\frac{1}{2}$ tsp roasted cumin seeds
2 flat dessert spoons of mango chutney
juice of 1 lemon
salt to taste

This side dish may be served as an accompaniment to any Indian meal but be warned, it's HOT!

Grind together in a blender or a spice grinder all the ingredients except the lemon juice, mango chutney and salt.
Season to taste with the salt, then add lemon juice and mango chutney and mix thoroughly.

Very easy, absolutely delicious, but eat with caution!!!

Catching up with the fastest man on the planet is not an easy task, but Racey Recipes managed to spend some precious moments with this quite remarkable man. Andy who is used to flying Tornado F3 jet-fighters, Mach 2 at 30,000 feet told RR that in Thrust SSC he was travelling at Mach 1 at 10 inches design ride-height! As an RAF jet fighter pilot, he is trained to withstand 4 to 5G even up to 6G, therefore the 1G he pulled in his supersonic car was not a problem to him although he found Eugine O'Brien's instruction at Silverstone's racing school "tremendously valuable" in learning how to assess a vehicle's limit and corrective measures when over the limit!! Lessons put to good effect when controlling SSC at 763 miles per hour! We asked him which experience had given him the maximum adrenaline kick, so far - he replied: "For sheer excitement and terror, it has to be as front man on the RAF bobsleigh team going down the Cresta Run, where your face is 3 inches off the ground as you are barrelling along the ice!"

On the rare occasions Andy has the time he enjoys cooking, especially curries when he usually cooks 2 or 3 different types, with different breads and his chilli pickle. "I like it because it is quick and simple to make and very tasty. It can also be used as a delicious starter if you cook the chillies carefully and the ones I prefer to use are the Hungarian variety."   Finally, when asked about the teams' eating habits in the desert, he said that breakfast was either a full English fry-up or cereals and fruit at 4am for their first run. Lunch would be sandwiches, fruit and fruit juice or water and, as the team was sponsored by several supermarkets, the evening meal would be similar to what would be eaten at home. During his normal working day, he often eats a couple of bars of chocolate plus fruit juice and then he will eat pasta and salad for his evening meal.

Castrol

The Liquid Engineers

100 years

Lubrication solutions since 1899

1979 Formed Eddie Jordan Racing (EJR)
1987 EJR won the Formula 3 Championship (Driver: Johnny Herbert)
1989 EJR won the Formula 3000 Championship (Driver: Jean Alesi)
1991 Formed Jordan Grand Prix
Grand Prix Wins: 1 (Damon Hill at the Belgian Grand Prix)

EDDIE AND MARIE JORDAN

WARM IRISH POTATO AND BLACK PUDDING SALAD

Eddie Jordan, Team Principal, Jordan Grand Prix

One of the great characters in the pitlane Eddie started his career as a successful driver before moving into team management. EJ has injected colour and a real buzz to the intensely competitive and sometimes clinical world of Formula 1. In 1998 he realised a dream when Damon Hill won Jordan's maiden Grand Prix victory at Spa whilst Ralf Schumacher's second position secured their place in the record books. Recently announced during the 1999 Monaco Grand Prix weekend, Eddie Jordan is the Tourism Sporting Ambassador for Ireland.

This recipe from Ireland is a favourite of Eddie's and is similar to one served at the Cherwell Boathouse Restaurant in Oxford.

Place potatoes in cold salted water, bring to the boil then simmer until tender. Approx 15/20 minutes.

Drain, cool slightly. Peel potatoes and slice into 5mm (¼ inch) slices. Toss potatoes in small bowl with the vinaigrette, shallots and parsley. Season with salt and pepper.

Heat large frying pan over a moderate heat, add oil and sliced black pudding, cook for 3 minutes on each side. Add to potatoes.

While the black pudding is cooking, drop broccoli florets in a pan of lightly salted water to boil for 4 minutes. Drain thoroughly and add to potatoes.

To serve, gently toss the potatoes with the broccoli and black pudding. Spoon on to warmed serving plates. Finish with gravy and chives.

You can substitute sausage, bacon and mushrooms and serve on a bed of lettuce.

Serves 6
12 small salad potatoes
175ml (6 fl oz) vinaigrette
2 shallots, finely diced
1 tblsp chopped fresh parsley
salt and pepper
1½ tblsp vegetable oil
450g (1lb) black pudding cut into 1 cm (½ inch) slices
350g (12oz) broccoli florets
5 tblsp meat gravy (optional)
1½ tblsp chopped fresh chives

HILL MILKMAN- DO YOU WANT SEMI-SK'D

GOAT'S CHEESE SALAD AND SPINACH & GOAT'S CHEESE TART

Drummer with Pink Floyd
Historic Car Racer and Collector

Nick Mason inherited a life-long passion for motorsport from his father. When the Pink Floyd drummer is nor performing in concerts around the world, he can pursue his passion for sports and racing cars and drive any number of mouthwatering machinery from his priceless collection. Nick has been racing regularly for the past twenty years and has competed at Le Mans 24-Hours five times.

Skye Gore was my tutor and gave me this recipe.

Make dressing in the blender adding the oil last.

For the salad:

Use Lollo Rosso, Oakleaf, Cos and Maché. Washed and dried. These can be refrigerated until needed.

Small round Crotin, suitable for grilling.

Approx. 4 pears, peeled and quartered. Cover with juice of 1 lemon to prevent discolouring.

Assembly:

Dribble olive oil on cheeses and grill to golden.

Toss salad with dressing and top with thin sliced pears (keeping pear shape). Top with grilled cheeses.

GOAT'S CHEESE SALAD
Goat's cheese
4 pears
mixed salad leaves
juice of a lemon
olive oil
For the dressing:
1/2 a cup of clear honey
1 cup of fine chopped fresh mint
juice of 4 limes
1/2 a cup of walnut oil
1 cup of vegetable oil
1 clove garlic
salt and pepper

SPINACH AND GOAT'S CHEESE TART

Pastry:
1 egg yolk
250g plain flour
125g unsalted butter
salt and pepper
1 tsp of dried or fresh marjoram

Filling:
1 bunch of cleaned and trimmed
(no stems) spinach
1 medium onion or small bunch spring onions
2 eggs, 2 egg yolks
1 cup cream
grated nutmeg
1 clove garlic
1 pinch of dry marjoram or 2 tblsp fresh
2 large Goat's cheese or 5 Crotin, approx. 1/2 lb.

Make the pastry, chill, roll into tart pan, prick and return to fridge for at least 15 mins.
Melt a little butter in pan and sweat onions.
Add spinach and let it wilt.
Sprinkle on the marjoram, garlic and seasoning.
Remove from heat.
Beat together the eggs, yolks, cream, nutmeg and half the Goat's cheese.
Line the bottom of the tart case with the spinach and pour on custard.
Sprinkle remaining cheese on top and bake for 20 - 25 minutes at 200C.
Top should be golden and custard set.

1965 Indy Car Champion, Rookie of the Year' Indy 500, USAC National Champion
1966 Indy Car Champion, USAC National Champion
1967 Won NASCAR 500, Won Sebring 12 Hour co-driving with Bruce McLaren
1969 Indy Car Champion, Won Indy 500, USAC National Champion
1978 Formula One World Champion, Team Lotus
1984 Indy Car Champion, Newman-Haas
Number of Indy Car wins: 52
Number of Grand Prix wins: *12
*Qualified on pole for debut race US Grand Prix (Team Lotus)

MARIO ANDRETTI

IDAHO POTATO GNOCCHI WITH BROWN SAUCE

Hardwick/Sutton

Just seconds after his blistering run up the famous Goodwood Hillclimb (1998 Festival of Speed), Mario confessed that gnocchi, made by his Mother, was one of his favourite dishes. "It must be made with Idaho potatoes" he insisted, "and served with brown sauce." Although he did not divulge his mother's recipe we believe they would both approve of this one. It could also be served with pesto or tomato sauce. A delicious starter.

Simmer the potatoes in lightly salted, boiling water for about 20 minutes or until tender. Drain, peel, mash and sieve them.

Mix the potatoes with ½oz/15g butter. Add the flour, egg, salt, pepper and nutmeg to taste. Work the mixture into a firm dough adding a little extra flour if the dough is too wet.

Chill for 1 hour.

Form the dough into small cylindrical shapes with floured hands.

Bring a large pan of lightly salted water to the boil and gently lower the gnocchi into the water and simmer for about 5 minutes or until they rise to the surface.

Meanwhile melt the remaining butter.

Lift the gnocchi out carefully using a slotted spoon and place on a heated serving dish. Pour the melted butter over the top and sprinkle with freshly grated Parmesan cheese.

For Brown Sauce

Heat the butter in a thick bottomed saucepan. Add the onion and stir until golden. Stir in the flour and cook over a low heat for 1 to 2 minutes until the mixture is a good golden brown colour. Remove the pan from the heat and gradually stir in the brown stock. Return the pan to the heat and bring to the boil, stirring. Boil for 5 minutes, skimming off any scum with a slotted spoon. Add carrots, turnip, mushrooms, celery, tomatoes (or purée) bouquet garni, garlic and black peppercorns.

Simmer the sauce gently for 1 hour, stirring occasionally and skimming when necessary. Strain the sauce through a fine sieve into a clean pan.

Leave it to stand for a few minutes to allow any fat to rise to the surface and skim it off.

Add salt to taste.

Reheat the sauce before serving with the gnocchi.

This sauce can be stored in a refrigerator for several days.

Serves 4
1lb (450g) floury Idaho potatoes
salt and freshly ground black pepper
2½oz (65g) butter
4oz (100g) flour or more if necessary, plus flour for flouring hands
1 small egg, beaten
freshly grated nutmeg
2oz (50g) freshly grated Parmesan cheese

BROWN SAUCE
1oz (25g) butter
1 small onion, thinly sliced
½oz (15g) or 2tbsp flour
1¼ pints (700ml) good brown stock
1 small carrot, sliced
1 small turnip, sliced
4 mushrooms, sliced
1 celery stalk, sliced
2-4 tomatoes, sliced or 1 to 2tbsp tomato purée
1 bouquet garni
2 cloves of garlic
12 black peppercorns, add salt to taste

ALAN MINSHAW

CAESAR SALAD

Founder & Chairman of Demon Tweeks
1974 Won British Production Saloon Car Championship, Hillman Avenger
1983 Class winner and Overall Runner-up British Saloon Car Championship, VW Golf GTi
1998 Won 2-Hour GT race at Imola, E-type Jaguar with his son, Jason.

Alan Minshaw has won over 150 combined overall and class wins during his racing career. He is currently campaigning a Maserati Birdcage T61 in the BRDC 50s Sports Car Championship, with occasional drives in a Lister Chevrolet, which is usually raced by Jason. Alan also races an E-type Jaguar in the Gentleman Drivers' Championship, comprising of 2-Hour endurance races at different circuits throughout Europe. Out of his seven children, his three sons Jon, Jason and Guy have all inherited his passion for motor racing and all successfully compete in various formulae. With a family of this size, Alan is not averse to concocting a delicious family meal in a respectable qualifying time.

Serves 4 - 6
1 cos lettuce
1x 50g/2oz can anchovies in olive oil, drained
1 small loaf rustic bread or ciabbatta
75g/3oz butter, melted
3 tblsp freshly grated Parmesan cheese

Dressing:
5 tblsp mayonnaise, preferably home-made
4 - 5 tblsp water
1 - 2 garlic cloves
freshly ground sea salt and black pepper

To make the dressing, put the mayonnaise in a bowl and stir in enough water to make a thin, pourable sauce.

Crush the garlic to a paste with a little salt.

Add to the mayonnaise with the Parmesan and stir.

Thin with a little more water if necessary so the sauce remains pourable.

Add pepper to taste.

Tear the lettuce into large pieces and place in a salad bowl.

Snip the anchovies into small pieces and sprinkle over lettuce.

To make the croutons, cut the bread into thick slices and remove the crusts.

Cut into 3cm/1inch cubes.

Toss in the melted butter and make sure all the cubes are coated.

Brush a baking sheet with some butter and arrange the cubes of bread on it.

Bake in a pre-heated oven 200C/400F/Gas mark 6 for about 12 minutes or until crisp and golden. Watch carefully as they can burn easily.

To serve, add the hot croutons to the salad bowl and drizzle the dressing over the salad. Finally sprinkle the Parmesan over the top.

PETER BROCK

VEGETABLE FILO PARCELS

9 times winner of Australian Bathurst 500
3 times Australian Touring Car Champion
Won 35 races during his racing career.

1 packet of filo pastry

mushrooms

1 onion

garlic to taste

a bunch of spinach

White Sauce:

plain flour

butter

soya or oat milk

grated hard cheese

seeded mustard

Clean the mushrooms and peel if necessary.

Chop the onion finely, crush the garlic.

Sauté the mushrooms, onion and garlic in a little olive oil or butter.

Wash and de-stalk the spinach, chop and sauté until wilted.

Make a white sauce: melt butter, add flour and cook briefly, add milk slowly, stirring to avoid lumps forming. Add mustard and grated cheese.

Season to taste.

The mixture should not be too runny.

Add the sautéed vegetables to the sauce.

Place a sheet of filo on the work surface (do not let it dry out) place some of the vegetables and sauce mixture and fold the pastry to make a parcel.

Bake in a pre-heated oven 180C for approx 30 minutes or until golden brown.

Serve with steamed honey and pepper carrots and steamed broccoli.

BERNIE AND SLAVICA ECCLESTONE

SATARAS (SATARASH)

Bernie Ecclestone, Chief Executive Officer, Formula One Administration Ltd
Vice-President, Fédération Internationale de l'Automobile, Promotional Affairs

1 large onion

18oz (500g) peppers

14oz (400g) tomatoes

1 tblsp sugar

4 tblsp oil

1 tblsp Vegata

salt and pepper

Sataras is a dish prepared from summer vegetables, primarily tomatoes, peppers and onion. The vegetables are diced with a special knife called a 'satara.'

It is a very simple dish to prepare, but very refreshing and has a delicious taste.

Sauté the sliced onion in oil, add sugar, cut the peppers into small strips and add to the pan.

Continue cooking until the peppers have softened a little. The dish is tastier if the peppers remain firm, so use as wide a pan as possible to help the liquid to evaporate quickly.

Add peeled and diced tomatoes and the Vegata. Continue cooking until all the liquid evaporates. Season to taste.

DON GRANT

GRAVADLAX NO COOKING COOKING.

Artist and Designer. Son of Gregor Grant, Founder of Autosport and
Eba Grant, Hon. Secretary, The Doghouse Owners' Club
and his sister
SIMONE GRANT
Photographer and Designer

GRAVADLAX

1 kg (2 lbs) of filleted middle cut salmon

2 handfuls of fresh dill, 1 tblsp of sea salt

1 tblsp demerara sugar, 1 tsp cooking brandy

1½ tablespoons of freshly ground black pepper

Check there are no bones remaining and leave the skin on, if possible.

Open up the fillet and lay it flat on some baking foil.

Having taken the stalks off the dill, place half of it on the fish, sprinkle on
the sugar, salt, pepper and brandy. Close the fish.

Make a parcel of the foil and place in a flat dish.

Next put a heavy weight (a house brick will do) onto a plate, which in
turn sits neatly within the dish. Place in the bottom of the fridge or a cool
larder.

During the next day and a half, turn the fish over, replacing the dill at
half time.

To serve: When the time is up, slice thinly and serve with brown bread
and a squeeze of lemon. Some people favour dill sauce, which is easier
to buy by the jar than make by the pint but this can swamp the delicate
taste of the fish.

Wash down with a bottle of Cortonn-Charlemagne, bought with the
money you have saved, or if you are feeling particularly Scandinavian, a
cold slug of Aquavit.

---

*You can make this delicious dish for a fraction of the cost of buying it. Personally,
I think it tastes better than all but the best wild Scottish smoked salmon. Not
only does it involve no cooking or even smoking, it is almost as straightforward
as putting something in the fridge.*

*I was first introduced to gravadlax, somewhat informally, by TIMO MAKINEN
in a bar in Monaco. He was drowning his sorrows with the help of industrial
quantities of Aquavit after the 1966 Monte Carlo rally, which resulted in the
Mini Cooper S's being disqualified by the beastly French on a technicality.*

HERB AND DOREEN JONES

GAZPACHO WITH A KICK AND RUSSIATINI

He quotes his dear friend 'Jenks' by saying that he was a racing motorist
Competed in the U.S. with C type Jaguar and in Europe with A.C. Team for 2
years and 1 year with a 2 litre Maserati
U.S.A.C. member
Doreen is a Doghouse member

GAZPACHO with a kick

Serves 4

4 tomatoes

1 small onion

a pinch of dried oregano

1 tblsp olive oil

garlic (optional)

2 tins of best chicken consommé soup or good chicken stock

½ tblsp white wine vinegar

salt and fresh ground black pepper

Finely chop the onion.

Drop the tomatoes into boiling water to loosen the skin, peel, de-seed and
remove core.

Chop the tomatoes. Add the vinegar, oregano, oil and seasoning (and
crushed garlic).

This is easiest to do in a food processor but can also be done by hand.

Mix well with the consommé or stock and chill in the refrigerator for at
least 2 hours before serving.

THE KICK. Before serving stir in a measure of vodka for each serving.

RUSSIATINI

Wipe the inside of a cocktail glass with a cut clove of garlic.

In a cocktail shaker sprinkle some freshly ground black pepper.

Add ice then a measure of your favourite vodka and 3 drops of dry
vermouth.

Stir don't shake. James Bond was wrong!

Serve with an olive.

HOWDEN GANLEY

Director of British Racing Drivers' Club (BRDC), Director of Silverstone Circuits Ltd.,
Consultant to Premier Fuel Systems Ltd., Secretary of BRDC
Chairman, Maidenhead Golf Club

Sylvia Davis

Starting out as a sporting journalist with the Waikato Times in his native New Zealand, Howden dovetailed his successful and varied racing career with designing and engineering racing cars from Formula 1 to CanAm and championship winning cars in a number of categories. In between cooking scrummy barbecue dishes (just try his Barbecued Vegetables or Spicy Potatoes) and consultancy work, or as Secretary of the BRDC, there is little time for a snooze in the bunker!

"I am into doing the barbecuing in this household so my culinary skills are generally restricted to anything that can be done on a grill or hot plate. Herself does the gourmet cooking."

SPICY POTATOES

Use larger new potatoes, $\frac{1}{2}$ lb per person. Adjust the quantity up or down according to your diet, or, if you are a Formula One driver, your trainer's instruction!

Peel the potatoes, cube them into .625 inch blocks. For non-engineers that is about the thickness of your thumb. I prefer them peeled, Judy prefers them just scrubbed. I think they taste better when I am the chef!

Place the cubed potatoes in a glass pyrex dish.

Drizzle the olive oil over the potatoes, then stir thoroughly to ensure that they are completely oiled.

Sprinkle the crushed peppers and the minced garlic over the oiled potatoes. Stir thoroughly and repeat.

I am fairly heavy handed with both peppers and garlic but you can adjust to suit your taste. You can mix them better with your hands, just DON'T LICK YOUR FINGERS AFTERWARDS!

Place in the oven and cook at Gas mark 6/170C for one hour, turning the cubes half way through the process.

They will emerge golden brown, slightly crisp.

Makes a wonderful accompaniment to most meals, particularly barbecues.

BARBECUED VEGETABLES

Remove the ends of the courgettes. Slice them into quarters lengthways. For that reason it is best to buy the straightest courgettes you can find. It is more difficult to slice down a curved one. (Stop laughing, Sylvia.)

Cut the aubergines lengthways into .375 thick slices. For non-engineers that is about the thickness of your little finger.

Pour sufficient sunflower oil into a glass dish, (needs a bit of judgement) and into the oil sprinkle enough of the various salts and peppers so that the mixture is thickened but still moist enough to coat the sliced vegetables. Turn the vegetables over and through the mixture and rub more mixture into the faces of the courgettes and aubergine. It is safe to lick your fingers afterwards! Leave the vegetables in the dish for at least one hour (preferably two) before cooking to ensure that they are well oiled and have absorbed the flavours.

Barbecue on a hot grill, turning regularly until lightly browned. You can cook them on the hot plate (assuming you have one on your barbie) but you miss the nice browned lines if you do them that way.

Serve with any barbecued meats or fish.

You can do the same with sweetcorn or asparagus (not sliced). Blanch the asparagus before oiling and seasoning. Cook the asparagus on the barbie hot plate.

BARBECUED VEGETABLES
courgettes (1 or 2 per person)
aubergines (egg plant if you are American)
sunflower oil
lemon and pepper salt
garlic salt
black pepper
Krazy Mixed Up Pepper
(if you are not able to buy this, it is just a mixture of several different types of pepper. Make your own!)

SPICY POTATOES
extra virgin olive oil
crushed red chilli peppers
minced garlic (or granules)
$\frac{1}{2}$lb potatoes per person

SPECIAL ROASTED RED PEPPERS

5 times Winner Le Mans 24 Hours
1968 – 1974 Formula 1 Driver: Ferrari, McLaren, Brabham, Surtees, Techno
GT Driver: Porsche, Ferrari, Nissan, Chevrolet, McLaren
1985 World Endurance Champion

Sporting Pictures UK

4 large red peppers, 1 per person,
look for 4 sided ones
4 medium tomatoes
2 garlic cloves
8 anchovy fillets (tinned), drained
8 dstsp of extra virgin olive oil
fresh ground black pepper

Cut the peppers in half and remove seeds, leave the stalks as they look nice when served.

Lay the peppers in a shallow roasting tray (lightly oiled) you should have 8 halves.

Blanch the tomatoes (approx. 1 minute). Remove skins, cut into quarters and place 2 quarters in each pepper half.

Slice the garlic cloves very thinly and divide among the peppers.

Cut the anchovy fillets into very small bits, one per pepper half.

Pour the olive oil over each pepper half and sprinkle with pepper.

Do not use salt – the anchovies give plenty of salt flavour.

Put them in the oven on a high shelf to roast for about an hour.

When done, serve with any juices from the tray poured over the top.

Garnish with basil and serve with lots of warm crusty bread - French or Italian - for soaking up the juices.

It's an unnerving business having breakfast with a Formula 1 driver. Just as you prepare to get stuck into a full English fry-up, toast and tea, a po-faced nutritional adviser will gently place a bowl of lumpy wallpaper paste in front of the driver as if this is a dish from La Gavroche.

These drivers are cool customers, and no mistake. Without so much as an envious glance in your direction, without the merest hint of a dribble as the smell of cooked bacon wafts across the table, they will eat the wallpaper paste and not say a word.

Problem is, of course, that speech is next to impossible as this confection of sawdust and horse oats, bound together by Polycell, has the effect of acting like super glue.

So don't even think about attempting an interview over breakfast. Play the tape back later and it sounds like the pole position winner is pissed and hasn't seen food for a fortnight. Either that or he's doing a poor imitation of a cow chewing the cud.

"Show, practish washn't show bad." Chew, chew, chew, chew. "Ha a bit ov unneersheer an"...chew, chew, chew, chew, chew.... "no trashon outda the sloe corneerzz. Abshalootly no glip. Ozzerwise"... chew, chew, chew, chew....... "everysing okay".

The dietitian, looking on like a proud father, will talk of vitamins and protein and a large fee for his trouble. Then he will present his man with a plastic bottle filled with a liquid which resembles something Linford Christie left behind in the sample room at Crystal Palace. And, just to make sure no one steals it (or pours it in a radiator, more like), the bottle carries the driver's name. Makes you wonder why he didn't also get a plastic bib with Thomas the Tank Engine across the front.

You want to ask what the hell is wrong with a plate of sausage, egg and beans? Okay, these seat harnesses being what they are, perhaps it's best to skip the beans. But, what about a piece of black pudding and a double helping of fried bread washed down by a mug of tea? Where's the harm in that?

How on earth did Fangio and Moss cope without having someone specially prepare their Marmite sandwiches and cocoa? Who was around in those days to add a sliver of snorting bull testicle and three drops of ram's bladder extract to their bacon butties? Just tell me that.

Before you do, kindly pass the full-cream butter and brown sauce, there's a dear.

MAURICE HAMILTON
Journalist, the Observer/BBC Radio 5 Live

Larger-than-life television celebrity once of the BBC Top Gear fame. Jeremy has now branched out to host his own chat show and is currently working on several other new TV projects. His outrageous and witty interview technique has turned many motor manufacturers into quivering wrecks as they wait for approval of their latest model. No wonder Jeremy's Cucumber Mousse is prone to suffering from the wobbles!!

Oil ring mould.

Peel and dice cucumber finely, sprinkle with salt and press between two plates for 30 minutes.

Sprinkle gelatine over cold water and leave until spongy.

Grate onion and mix with the cheese and seasoning.

Whip cream and put in fridge.

Pour boiling stock over gelatine and stir until dissolved. Cool.

Drain cucumber. Mix with vinegar, sugar and spices.

Add the gelatine to the cheese mix. Add cucumber, lastly fold in cream.

Pour into a mould and leave overnight.

Bring to room temperature 1 hour before turning out.

Fill the centre of the ring with prawns and garnish with watercress and green pepper slices.

1 large cucumber
6oz (180g) curd or cream cheese
1/2 onion
1/2 oz gelatine soaked in 3 tblsp cold water
1/4 pint vegetable or chicken stock
2 tblsp white wine vinegar
1 tblsp caster sugar
pinch of ground mace / coriander
1/4 pint double cream, whipped until it forms thin ribbons
1 1/2 - 2 pint capacity ring mould
vegetable oil
salt and pepper
prawns, watercress and /or green peppers to garnish

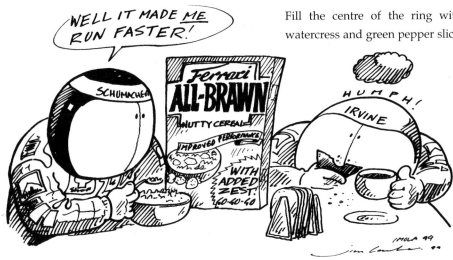

PHIL HILL

FRESH MOZZARELLA

First American Formula 1 World Champion (Ferrari, 1961)

David Hayhoe

1958-1964 Formula 1 Driver: Maserati, Ferrari, Cooper, ATS, Lotus
1961 Formula 1 World Champion with Ferrari
Grand Prix wins: 3 (first win 1960 Italian GP with Ferrari)
1958, 1961, 1962, Won Le Mans 24 Hours, with Olivier Gendebien, Ferrari
1955 Won US National Sports Car Championship, Ferrari
Won sports car races at Buenos Aires and Sebring, 1958, Ferrari.
Won sports car races 1961 Sebring and Le Mans.
Won sports car race 1000 kms Nurburgring and a CanAm race.

After he retired as a professional racing driver in 1967, Phil concentrated on his Classic Restoration business in California, building it into a highly successful enterprise, which he sold years later. He currently enjoys guest appearances at historic racing events and overseeing his son, David's single-seater racing career.

American race ace, Phil Hill kindly took some time out of his busy schedule of testing and reacquainting himself with the Shelby and beautiful "Sharknose" Ferrari, during the Goodwood Circuit Revival Meeting, to divulge his love of Fresh Mozzarella

"My favourite food is fresh mozzarella cheese! You know" he added, clearly reliving the moments of preparation of his favourite dish, "it comes in a ball and when you remove the wrapper the smell is wonderful, so fresh! Then you slice it carefully and lay it like a fan on a large oval serving dish. Just drizzle some good olive oil on top and grind some fresh black pepper over it and it's beautiful," he kissed his fingers, looked to heaven and said: "Formidable! Normally we could only get the real fresh mozzarella in Italy, but now, just recently, a couple of Italian guys have started making it in the U.S. and it's just the same wonderful texture, flavour and smell. In fact the L.A. Times have just done an article on these guys and their Mozzarella."

Phil enjoys the dish any time of the day, in fact, it seemed to be the only food that passes his lips, although he later confessed to a liking for Treacle Tart served with fresh cream.

Does your wife make it for you we asked: "No, my wife says that I can't have it any more, as it will clog up my already clogged up arteries!"

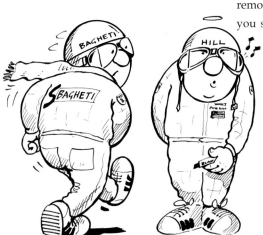

TIGELLA, PINZIMONIO AND AFFETTATO

Formula 1 Designer: March Engineering, Hesketh Racing, Wolf Racing, Ferrari, Tyrrell and Sauber

Phipps/Sutton

"As you know I lived and worked in Italy for many years during the 1980s and in August, the hottest month of the year, everything normally shuts down and everyone goes to the seaside. The Italian cuisine is very regionalised and varies greatly from province to province. During the month of August it was traditional in the province of Modena for those few restaurants which remained open to serve only one dish which was traditional to the area and perfect for the hot summer evenings. It is called Tigella and consists of tigellas which are small round breads, pinzimonio, which are sticks of fresh vegetables and an affettato which is a plate of finely sliced salumi.

The Pinzimonio are very fresh sticks of celery, carrots, peppers or anything else which is crispy and in season.

Finally the plate of salumi would consist of thinly sliced prosciutto, salami, coppa, mortadella and speck. On the table would also be freshly grated parmesan cheese, balsamic vinegar, olive oil and salt. There would also be lardo which is lard or butter mixed with fresh garlic and rosemary.

The meal begins by preparing in individual bowls a mixture of olive oil, balsamic vinegar and salt to make a dip. The tigellas then arrive hot on the table, you slice the tigella open, spread it with lardo, sprinkle on fresh parmesan, fold in a slice of prosciutto or salami, dip it and eat it followed by the sticks of fresh vegetables also dipped in the vinegar.

The meal is totally delicious and everybody normally eats far more than they anticipated. The whole thing should be washed down with bottles of foaming Lambrusco (the bottle should never have a label) and when you can eat no more, a cone of lemon ice cream and expresso coffee should round the meal off perfectly.

If you are worried about indigestion, follow the meal with a good grappa or nocino."

One of Britain's most talented designers and engineers whose innovative ideas revolutionised Grand Prix racing. The Postlethwaite designed Wolf won its maiden Grand Prix and he led Ferrari to two constructors' titles. Harvey's infectious enthusiasm and passion for racing and engineering was inspirational to everyone who knew him.

Harvey died just before Racey Recipes was published.

We enclose the recipe he gave us because we feel it reflects his love of Italy, his appreciation of food and his joie de vivre.

Tigellas are made from flour, water, cream, milk, salt and yeast which are mixed together and allowed to rise for a couple of hours. This would normally be made around midday for an evening meal. The dough is rolled out, cut into small squares and cooked using a padella which is a hot male and female mould held over a flame, which quickly cooks several tigellas at the same time. The good cook will produce a continuous flow of these during the meal, served in a small round basket.

PAUL EDWARDS

JACQUES VILLENEUVE'S BREAKFAST

Edwards Hospitality Services, catering for: Williams Grand Prix, Jordan Grand Prix, British American Racing, Bridgestone, Goodyear, Winfield Racing, Prodrive World Rally, TOCA and MSD Peugeot.

We cornered Paul at Silverstone and asked him what Jacques liked to eat, he replied that Jacques' main meal was actually breakfast, the only meal when he saw him sit down and physically eat. He said. . . . . . .

"As you probably know, he (Jacques) is a great fan of fresh milk and he does not like it from a jug – he likes to see it come from a carton out of the fridge. His other great passion is chocolate and if he has a particularly good day on the track, i.e. a win, he will scoff three to four chocolate bars down and drink possibly a pint of milk. That is his way of celebrating.

Going on to his favourite breakfast, he normally arrives at about 8.30 in the morning and will come straight into the kitchen and ask for what he calls French toast. Jacques' version of French toast is as follows:

Take three eggs and mix with salt, pepper and a couple of teaspoons of milk. Beat well until of equal consistency. Take three slices of bread, cut into half. Whilst preparing the eggs and bread, have the frying pan heating up with a mixture of oil and butter, just enough to brown the bread, but not to give it real colour. When this is sufficiently hot, i.e. not quite smoking, dip both sides of the bread in the egg/milk mixture and then slowly cook as you would ordinary fried bread.

He likes it slightly coloured but not well done, i.e. a slightly mouldy brown/yellowy look. This will take about 2 - 2½ minutes to cook – no longer. Cook one side and then turn over and cook the other.

This must be served with genuine Canadian maple syrup. We always get a supply of this in Montreal and carry it around with us to all the races and it has to be Canadian! He would put on a liberal amount of maple syrup and this would be his main meal. He would follow this with two lightly fried eggs and once again, possibly milk and toast with syrup. If he was so inclined, he may take the yoghurt/bird seed mixture that the dietition/physio would mix for him – but normally he preferred his own!

Regarding other meals, he was fairly easy to please. He would have pasta with tomato sauce – no garlic - but he would like it quite flavoursome with salt, pepper, onion etc and maybe some basil and sometimes he would have a fillet steak, medium rare; but these are a few of the meals we prepared for him, because as you know, he would normally have dinner in the hotel.

I hope this gives you a little insight into Jacques Villeneuve's eating habits!"

Paul Edwards can often be spotted on Grand Prix day, on the pit-wall hanging out the pit-board signals and times for the Williams drivers.

JACK MUNCH

HILL JACQUES HAS ATE YOUR HAMSTER

AL UNSER JNR

SHELLEY UNSER'S
VICTORY LANE QUESADILLAS

Champ Car Driver: Team Penske

1981 Won SCCA Super Vee title

1982 Won SCCA Can-Am Championship

1986 Won Daytona 24 Hours, IROC Champion

1987 Won Daytona 24 Hours

1988 IROC Champion

1990 CART PPG Indy Car Champion

1992 and 1994 Won Indy 500

Number of wins: 30+

With more than 30 victories in 14 years of Indy car racing, Little Al has proudly upheld the family racing tradition. His best season came in 1994 when he won eight of sixteen races, including the Indy 500, to take his second Indy Car World Series title.

Broil flour tortillas covered in cheese with chilli until bubbling. You may also cook on the top of stove in a pan.

Add favourite salsa.

Some people prefer to add ingredients of their choice and fold the tortilla in half to make it easier to eat!

This can be turned into a meal by adding any of the following: diced tomatoes, lettuce, shredded beef, chicken, guacamole, sour cream, black olives, onions or green peppers.

Serves 6 to 8
12 flour tortillas
1 lb Colby or Monterey cheese
salsa
green chilli (diced or whole)

FAVOURITE RESTAURANTS

SIR JACK BRABHAM
EDWINN's, Church Road, Shepperton, Middlesex.

CRAIG POLLOCK
MIROIR d'ARGENTINE, SOLALEX, SWITZERLAND.
This is a small restaurant run by two brothers (Jaeggi) at the end of a spectacular valley near Villars sur Ollon, a holiday resort in the French part of Switzerland. It is open from the end of May until the end of September and then becomes inaccessible due to snow. Their cuisine is outstanding and unique and well worth the trip.

OLIVIER PANIS
ESMERALDA, MONTREAL, CANADA.
This is Olivier's favourite restaurant although he has never been there! After his dreadful accident in the 1997 Canadian Grand Prix, ESMERALDA sent him a delicious meal to the hospital, it was his first proper meal after being hospitalised.

JARNO TRULLI
Jarno loves going to IL MORETTINO, PESCARA, ITALY.
He has been going there since he was a small child and his favourite dish is their fish soup.

DAVE CHARLTON
LA PERLE, Seapoint, Cape Town, South Africa

STEFAN JOHANSSON

Team Principal Johansson Motorsport - Indy Lights

1975-1996 Raced: Formula Ford, Formula 3, Formula 2, Formula 1, Indy Cars and Sports Cars.

1980 British Formula 3 Champion, Project Four, March

1983-1990 Formula 1 Driver: Spirit Honda, Tyrrell, Honda, Ferrari, McLaren, Ligier, Onyx

1991-1996 Indy Car Driver (1991) CART "Rookie of the Year"

1999 Sports Car Driver: to contest the Daytona 24 Hour Classic, Ferrari 333SP Doran Team

Stefan told Racey Recipes that his favourite food was 'sushi', which he discovered whilst racing in Japan. He enjoys a wide variety, and values its fresh, light qualities and the fact that it is so easy to digest.

KRISTIAN KOLBY

UK-based Danish Formula 3 driver who really enjoys fish, but insists it must be freshly caught from the sea. He loves a speciality of Fried Eel, as cooked by his Grandmother, and Rodspaette with remoulade (a type of tartar sauce), served with boiled potatoes and salad.

Kristian is a secret ice-cream lover. He sheepishly confessed to Racey Recipes: "I love all different types of ice-cream. I could eat it anytime, anywhere, and with almost anything."

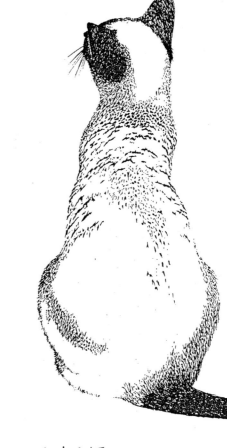

FLYING TONIGHT

DonGrant

DAN GURNEY

TROUT WITH ASPARAGUS AND NEW POTATOES

Formula 1 Driver, Indy Car Driver, Constructor

David Hayhoe

1959 – 1970 Formula 1 Driver: Ferrari, BRM, Porsche, Brabham, Eagle, McLaren
1961 3rd Formula 1 World Championship, Porsche
Grand Prix wins: 4 (one with Eagle)
1964 Constructor: Founded Eagle
1965 Formed (with Carroll Shelby): All-American Racers (IndyCar series)
1966 Formed Anglo-American Racers (Formula 1)
1967 First win: Race of Champions (F1), Brands Hatch, Eagle
Grand Prix win: Belgium, Eagle-Weslake
Won Le Mans 24 Hours with AJ Foyt, Ford GT Mark 4
1968 and 1969 runner-up Indy 500, Eagle; ('68 winner Bobby Unser, Eagle)
1990 Toyota backed Eagles entered sports car racing, in USA
1992/1993 Won IMSA series: Juan Manuel Fangio 11, Eagle

At the 1998 Goodwood Motor Circuit Revival Meeting, Dan was in no doubt as to what was his favourite meal.

White asparagus, cooked until just tender (about 5 minutes or less, depending on the size of the stalks) and then dressed with olive oil and vinegar.

Wild trout, straight out of the river, cleaned and pan fried in a little butter.

New potatoes, so small and new they don't need anything more than a quick wash, then steamed for 15 to 20 minutes, until tender and served with butter and a garnish of parsley.

1964 Formula 1 World Champion with Ferrari, Formula 1 Constructor

1956, 1958, 1959, 1960 500cc. Motor Cycle World Champion MV Agusta

1958, 1959, 1960 350cc. Motor Cycle World Champion MV Agusta

1966 CanAm Champion with Lola

1960-1972 Formula 1 Driver: Lotus, Cooper, Lola, Ferrari, Honda, BRM, McLaren, Surtees Grand Prix wins: 6

1960 Won his maiden race (in cars) at Goodwood (Cooper).

1970 Founded Team Surtees; finishing 7th in debut race (British GP); 5th (Canadian GP).

His outstanding career speaks for itself; JS is undoubtedly one of the greatest racing legends. John still enjoys his racing and makes several guest appearances at historic racing events around the globe. He is an active Patron of the Goodwood Festival of Speed and Goodwood Motor Circuit, where you can see him in action with a swarm of MV Agustas or driving a fabulous vintage Mercedes or Ferrari.

JOHN AND JANE SURTEES

CRAB CLAWS AND PRAWNS IN RED CURRY

John Surtees MBE
The only man to win a World Championship on two and four wheels

Simone Grant

John and Jane eat a lot of Thai food, this is one of their favourites.

Boil tin of coconut milk and the red curry paste and Kaffir leaves until it gives up it's oil (about 10-15 minutes).

Add all the other ingredients.

Cook just until the prawns and crab claws are hot, do not over cook.

Serve immediately.

Add coriander to garnish.
Serve with Thai rice.

Serves 2
1 tin of coconut milk
1 tsp of red curry paste
2 tblsp of Thai fish sauce
2 tblsp sugar
6oz shelled, frozen prawns
8 to 10 crab claws, depending on size
1 small tin of pineapple pieces
I sliced red pepper
4 Kaffir lime leaves, fresh or dried
coriander to garnish

Lynton Money

PAULINE HAILWOOD

TRUITE FARCIES BRETONNE

Wife of the late Mike Hailwood, Nine-times Motor-cycle World Champion,
Twelve-times winner IoM TT, won Senior IoM TT again in 1979
Formula 1 Driver: Reg Parnell Racing, Surtees, McLaren

TRUITE FARCIES BRETONNE
6 river trout
1 glass of white wine (3 ¾ fl oz)
1oz clarified butter

FARCE
8oz crab meat (this can be a
mixture of dark and light meat)
1oz butter
2 shallots, finely chopped
3 tblsp fresh white beadcrumbs
1 hard-boiled egg
1 egg yolk

TO FINISH
1oz butter
1 tblsp chopped parsley
mixed herbs
juice of ½ lemon

Split the trout down the back and remove the backbone carefully.

Prepare farce: soften shallots in the butter, add to the crab meat and mix with the crumbs, hard-boiled egg (chopped) and the yolk.
Season well and fill into the trout.
Lay in a fire-proof dish, pour over the wine and butter and cook in a moderate hot oven.
185C/375F/Gas mark 4 for 15 minutes.

Take out the trout, carefully place on a hot serving dish and keep warm.
Strain the cooking liquor, add the strained lemon juice, seasoning and herbs.
Heat a small frying pan, put in the remaining butter and cook to a 'noisette' then add the lemon and herbs. Spoon over the trout while still foaming and serve at once, garnished with parsley and lemon.

1989 French Formula Renault Champion
1992 and 1993 International Formula 3000
Champion, DAMS
1994 - 1999 Formula 1 Driver: Ligier, Prost
Grand Prix Wins: 1 (1996 Monaco)

OLIVIER PANIS

POACHED SALMON

Formula 1 Driver Prost

Prost GP

Find a big saucepan or borrow a fish kettle.

Half fill the pan with water and put in all the vegetables, salt, peppercorns and bouquet garni.

Boil gently for 30 mins to make a vegetable stock.

Clean and scale the fish.

Gently add the fish and cook until the flesh separates from the bone.

Do not overcook, salmon can be rather dry.

Serve hot with new potatoes and petit pois.

Serve cold with cucumber and salad.

Allow 6 oz (180g) per helping
for added flavour poach it in a court
bouillon, you will need:
1 small turnip
1 small onion
½ leek
1 stick of celery
peppercorns
bouquet garni

Sutton

LOBSTER

1972-1985 Formula 1 Driver: Brabham,
Surtees, Lotus, Penske, McLaren
Grand Prix Wins: 5

Wattie survived a lurid spin in front of the entire field, before bringing his McLaren home first and claiming his only British Grand Prix victory, and the first for McLaren under the new management and control of Ron Dennis. John narrowly missed winning the world championship honours, ending the 1982 season runner-up to Austrian ace, Niki Lauda. After a successful spell racing for Porsche (sportscar category), John set up his own Racing School at Silverstone, before embarking on a successful television commentary career.

When cornered at Silverstone John waxed lyrical about Irish seafood, particularly lobster, served with floury Irish potatoes and lots of Irish butter.

If you cook your own lobster you have, needless to say, to kill it yourself. There are many different views on the most humane way of doing this. The RSPCA guidelines suggest that you put the live lobster in the freezer for 30 minutes which will reduce it to a state of torpor. Then, pierce the body with a sharp knife through the cross on its back. It can then be boiled.

Better still, get someone else to do it for you!

Bring a large pan of water to the boil, put the lobster in the water and bring back to the boil and cook for 15 minutes.

Cut in half lengthways and remove the gills, the stomach sac and the intestines.

It is also possible to steam lobsters or grill them; you need to cut them in half before cooking if you do it this way.

Serve á la Watson with floury potatoes and lots of butter or alternatively with mayonnaise.

BBC Top Gear's Celebrity Test-Driver, GT Sports Car Driver, 1975 Formula Ford 1600 Champion , 1976 Won the Grovewood Award, 1980 Formula 1 Driver: Ensign Also Japanese Formula 2, Touring Cars, Procar series and Sports Cars, Journalist and broadcaster, Top Gear BBC Television.

Forget your pizza delivery rider, when it comes to fast food Tiff Needell is your man. A veteran of one Grand Prix (well two dozen laps of the 1980 Belgian Grand Prix), Tiff has recently entered the Guinness Book of Records. Driving a McLaren F1 sportscar, Tiff set the fastest ever production car lap time at a British track, when he averaged 195mph around the Millbrook Bowl.

LOBSTER THERMIDOR	FOR THE MORNAY SAUCE	FOR THE BERCY REDUCTION
4 small live lobsters		
3 tblsp oil	$3/4$ oz (20g) butter	1 tblsp chopped shallot
1 oz (30g) butter	$3/4$ oz (20g) flour	$1/4$ lb (110g) clarified butter
1 tsp Dijon mustard	$1/2$ pint (290ml) milk	1 glass white wine
1 level tsp grated	2 tblsp fresh grated	
Parmesan cheese	Parmesan cheese	
browned crumbs	salt, pepper and cayenne	

Make the mornay sauce, melt the butter, add the flour and cook for 1 minute.
Remove from heat and add the milk.
Return to heat and slowly bring to the boil, stirring well until you have a creamy sauce.
Season with salt, pepper and cayenne and simmer for 3 minutes.
Remove from heat, add the Parmesan and adjust the seasoning.
Preheat oven to 180C/350F/Gas mark 4.
Place the lobster in the deep freeze until they are torpid. Pierce the cross on the back of their head with a sharp knife right through the nerve centre. This will kill them instantly. Split the lobsters in half lengthways, remove the little stomach sac from near the head and the dark intestines.
Heat the oil and butter and sauté the lobsters, flesh side down for 5 minutes then put it in the oven for 15 minutes (make sure the handle won't melt).
Soften the shallot in the clarified butter over gentle heat until soft and transparent.
Add the wine and boil fast until reduced to 3 tablespoons. Mix this bercy reduction and the liquid from the lobster pan with the mornay sauce.
Heat it up and add the mustard.
Remove all the meat from the lobster shells. Chop up the meat from the claws and the creamy flesh from the head. Cut the tail meat into scallops.
Mix the chopped meat with some of the sauce and pile it into the shells.
Put scalloped meat on top and coat with remaining sauce and sprinkle with cheese and crumbs.
Place in the oven to reheat and then brown under grill. Serve 2 half lobsters per person.

Loti Irwin

PAELLA AUX FRUITS DE MER

Formula 1 Driver: Jordan
1994 – '98 Formula 1 Driver: Sauber and Williams
Grand Prix wins: 1

Heinz-Harald's mother makes wonderful paella which has been his favourite since he can remember. Heinz-Harald keeps it as a closely guarded secret and did not 'spill the beans' so the following recipe is a combination of what HH told us and one of our own favourite recipes, see if you agree..

Optional: you can add more and different seafood if available. Lobster, monk fish or calamari would be delicious.

Cook the mussels in a little water for about 5 minutes, discard any that are not open.

Set aside.

In a large saucepan with a lid cook the onions (chopped) and peppers (finely sliced) in a little oil until soft.

Add the rice, herbs to taste, saffron, salt and pepper. Stir to coat the rice with oil.

Add the beans, peas, tomatoes (chopped) and stock and wine mixed with the mussel water to make 1 ½ pints. Bring to the boil and simmer for 5 minutes, stirring occasionally.

When the rice is cooked and all the liquid has been absorbed add the prawns, replace the lid and cook for another 5 minutes.

Finally add the mussels and serve immediately.

If using other seafood, add with the prawns.

4 or 5 pints of mussels
1 pint of prawns
8oz (225g) rice (Arborio is best)
a glass of white wine
2 shallots or a small onion
1 clove of garlic
1 cup of peas, fresh or frozen
olive oil
black pepper
2 or 3 tomatoes
1 red or green pepper
a pinch of saffron
2 bay leafs
6oz (175g) fine green beans
fish stock (from a cube)

NONO, NO, HOW MANY TIMES DO I HAVE TO TELL YOU - YOU PUT THE EGGS IN FIRST & THEN THE SUGAR!!

BOUILLABAISSE

Drummer with Pink Floyd
Historic Car Racer and Collector

Skye Gore was my tutor and gave me this recipe.

1 ½ lbs monkfish
1 lb mackerel
1 quart fish stock made from:
mackerel bits from filleting.
Cover with water and bring
to the boil.
Simmer 15 minutes.
Strain and reserve.
1 large crab
½ cup of olive oil
1 medium onion, sliced
1 leek, sliced
1 celery stalk, sliced
1 large tomato, peeled, seeded and
chopped
3 cloves garlic
1 bouquet garni
strip of orange peel
½ chopped fennel bulb, top is best,
fronds could replace bulb
¼ tsp saffron
½ cup chopped parsley
seasoning
tomato paste
Pernod
croutons and Gruyere

Heat oil in a large pot and stir in onions, celery and leeks. Sweat.

Add stock, tomato, bouquet garni, garlic, orange peel and fennel.

Sprinkle in saffron, seasoning and simmer for 40 minutes (now make the Rouille).

Add mackerel and crab and boil hard for 7 minutes.

Don't stir and disturb but shake occasionally.
Lay white fish on top and boil for 5 minutes.
Rolling boil will emulsify oil.

Remove fish, whisk in tomato paste and Pernod.

Return fish, sprinkle on parsley.

Serve with croutons of toasted french bread, Gruyere and Rouille.

ROUILLE

1 slice of de-crusted bread
2 tablespoon water
1 chilli pepper, de-seeded
1 egg yolk
3 or 4 cloves of garlic
½ cup of olive oil
seasoning

Soak bread in 2 tablespoons water. Squeeze dry. Purée bread with chilli, egg yolk, salt and 2 tablespoon oil. With blender running trickle in remaining oil (as for mayonnaise).

GRILLED LANGOUSTINES WITH FENNEL AND CHILLI SAUCE

President of the Fédération Internationale de l'Automobile (FIA)

After competing successfully in European Formula 2, Max Mosley moved into administration and Formula 1 as a Founder Director of March Engineering, which ran a works Formula 1 team and supplied customer cars for F2, F3 and F5000. They won their first Grand Prix with Jackie Stewart at just their second attempt. Administration and organisational roles within the FISA and then the FIA beckoned the former barrister. As FIA chief, stringent safety measures to circuits, chassis and cockpit design have been implemented with several safety features adopted into passenger vehicles. Chairman of the European New Car Assessment Programme, the Euro NCAP crash test programme has transformed car safety.

Racey Recipes caught up with him at his London offices when he admitted that one of his favourite restaurants in London (for an off-duty lunch) was the RIVER CAFE…. This is their recipe, from The River Café Cook Book, published by Ebury Press. By Kind Permission of Ruth Rogers and Rose Gray.

Preheat grill to very hot.

Finely chop the green fennel tops and the fennel bulb and put in a bowl together with the chopped chilli. Add the lemon juice and leave for 5 to 10 minutes.

Add the olive oil and season with salt and pepper.

Grill the langoustines or prawns for 2 to 3 minutes on either side.

Serve with the lemon quarters and the sauce.

This sauce can be used with any grilled fish or chicken.

Serve with a mixed leaf salad and a basil-flavoured mayonnaise.

Mazzancolle ai Ferri
Serves 4
5 or 6 langoustines or
tiger prawns per person
lemon quarters

For the sauce
the green tops of 3 fennel bulbs
or 4 tblsp fresh fennel herb
1 small fennel bulb
2 whole fresh red chilli, seeded
and finely chopped
juice of 1 lemon
5 tblsp extra virgin olive oil
sea salt and freshly ground
black pepper

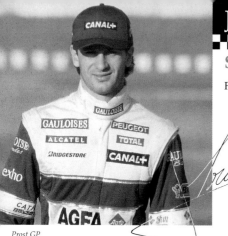

Prost GP

JARNO TRULLI

SQUID WITH PEAS IN TOMATO SAUCE

Formula 1 Driver Prost

1983-1995 Multiple Kart Champion
1995-1996 German Formula 3 Championship
1996 German Formula 3 Champion (Benetton Jnr. Team)
1997-1999 Formula 1 Driver: Minardi, Prost

2 ½ lbs (1.25kg) small squid
3 tomatoes
2 cloves of garlic
2 onions
1 cup of petit pois, fresh or frozen
¼ pint (150ml) olive oil
a small piece of orange peel
1 tblsp tomato purée
8 fl oz (250 ml) white wine
bouquet garni
1 egg yolk
salt and pepper

Optional 1 chilli

Clean the squid discarding all but the bodies and tentacles. Dry and cut into strips.

Peel the tomatoes (drop them into boiling water for 10 seconds) remove seeds and chop flesh coarsely.
Peel and chop the garlic and onions.

Heat 2 tablespoons of olive oil in a frying pan. Add the squid and cook over a high heat until all the moisture has evaporated. Add the onions, garlic and orange peel, cook for 3 minutes, stirring all the time.
Add the tomatoes, tomato purée, wine and bouquet garni (and chilli, if used).
Cover and simmer over a very low heat for 1½ hours.
Add a little water from time to time if necessary.

5 minutes before the end of cooking time add the peas and return to heat.
Put the egg yolk in a bowl and whisk in the remaining olive oil. Remove pan from heat and add the egg mixture to bind the sauce.

Discard the bouquet garni and serve immediately.

BOBBY RAHAL

Triple IndyCar World Series Champion 1986, 1987, 1992

Indy 500 winner 1986

1992 Formed Rahal/Hogan Racing

(winning the Champ Car title)

SCALLOP RAVIOLI IN SAFFRON CAVIAR SAUCE

First "Rookie" owner/driver to win champ car series (1992) with Rahal-Hogan Racing

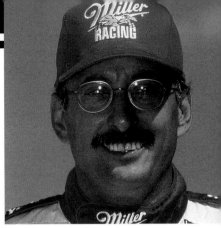

Hardwick/Sutton

Advance preparation.

Drop washed spinach leaves into 4 cups boiling water. Cook until wilted, drain, cool then mince. Combine spinach, carrots, green onions, ginger, scallops, chicken, sherry and pepper.

Mix thoroughly.

Within 5 hours of cooking, fold dumplings. Trim won tons into circles.

Place 2 tsp of filling in centre of each won ton.

Moisten the edge with water and fold dumpling in half.

Set aside caviar, chilli and chives. In a small bowl combine remaining ingredients.

Last minute (pit stop) cooking.

Pour cream mixture into 12 inch skillet. Bring to a vigorous boil and cook until the sauce thickens enough so the spoon leaves a path as the sauce is stirred (about 5 mins).

Turn heat down to lowest setting.

Bring 4 quarts of water to vigorous boil. Add the dumplings and give them a gentle stir.

When the dumplings float to the surface (about 3 mins) gently remove from water and drain.

Transfer dumplings to 4 to 8 serving plates.

Spoon the sauce over the top, sprinkle with chopped chives.

Decorate each plate with a little caviar and a dot of chilli sauce.

Serve at once.

Serves 4 to 8 as a starter, 2 as a main course

12oz spinach, stemmed
$\frac{1}{4}$ cup chopped carrots
1 green onion, minced
1 tblsp fresh ginger, finely minced.
$\frac{1}{2}$ lb bay scallops, minced
$\frac{1}{4}$ lb ground chicken
2 tblsp light soy sauce
2 tsp dry sherry
$\frac{1}{4}$ tsp white pepper
20 won ton skins
cornstarch for dusting

Sauce:
2 oz top quality black caviar
2 tblsp Chinese chilli sauce
1 bunch chives, minced
1 cup whipping cream
$\frac{1}{4}$ cup dry sherry
1 tsp dark sesame oil
$\frac{1}{4}$ tsp salt
pinch of saffron
2 tsp fresh ginger, finely minced

KARLSKOGA TROUT WITH CHILLED YOGHURT SAUCE

Titan Formula 3 Constructor, Entrant and Racer, Historic Driver
Loti's brother kindly gave us this recipe.

Karlskoga, Sweden 1966

It had not been a great weekend for C. Lucas Team Lotus as, not only had Chris Irwin won the race but our two drivers, Piers Courage and Roy Pike, had run into each other on the cooling down lap. Nevertheless, we went to the post race party in a large hut in the woods which was the usual subdued affair, although as time passed, the lack of music and the fair sex was increasingly noticed. So we sent Bubbles Horsley out into the woods with a loudhailer and a bottle to find some.

While he was away – and we expected he would be away for some time - we were served trout from the lake, which was baked in the oven wrapped in newspaper. Autosport for the smaller fish, Motoring News for the larger ones and the Financial Times for Jackie Stewart.

The fish was stuffed with herbs and a slice of lemon and wrapped in an envelope of two sheets of paper. They were soaked under the tap and placed in the oven 350F/180C/Gas mark 4 until the paper dried completely, about 8 to 10 minutes.

When the packages were slit open and the paper peeled back, the skin of the trout conveniently came away with it. Served with chilled a yoghurt sauce.

Delicious. Then a bus drew up outside. Bubbles had found the touring Pontefract Girls Brass Band – still in their uniforms. The evening was complete.

Happy days.

Yoghurt sauce

300 ml of plain yoghurt
3 tblsp of peeled chopped cucumber
1 tblsp of chopped chives
$\frac{1}{2}$ tsp of concentrated mint sauce
juice of $\frac{1}{2}$ lemon
salt and pepper

ADRIAN AND TANIA FERNANDEZ

STEAMED SALMON AND SPINACH WITH MUSHROOM AND CILANTRO SAUCE

Tania told Racey Recipes: "Maintaining the healthy diet that Adrian follows, makes it a little harder to make things taste good! This dish is one of his favourites and, is guilt free."

Champ Car Driver: Patrick Racing
1991 Mexican Formula 3 Champion
1992 'Rookie of the Year' Indy Lights Championship
1993-1999 Champ Car Driver: Galles Racing, Patrick Racing

Levitt/Sutton USA

METHOD

1. Reserve 4 cilantro sprigs for garnish. Coarsely chop remaining cilantro leaves and stems. Set aside. In 12 inch skillet heat olive oil over medium/high heat until hot. Add mushrooms and cook, stirring occasionally, until liquid evaporates and mushrooms are browned, about 10 minutes. Add broth (or stock) and vinegar; cook until liquid is reduced by half 2-3 minutes. Stir in soy sauce, margarine and brown sugar. Keep sauce warm.

2. Meanwhile, spray vegetable steamer with non-stick cooking spray; place in 5 quart Dutch oven. Add 1 inch of water; heat to boiling over high heat.

3. Sprinkle salmon with salt and pepper; place on steamer. Place spinach on top of salmon and cover Dutch oven. Cook 8-12 minutes until fish flakes easily when tested with a fork.

4. To serve, arrange spinach on 4 warm plates; place salmon on spinach. Stir cilantro into mushroom sauce. Spoon mushroom sauce over salmon. Garnish with reserved cilantro sprigs.

Makes 4 main dish servings
Prep: 15 minutes
Cooking time: about 20 minutes

1 large bunch of cilantro (coriander)
2 tblsp olive oil
8oz sliced mushrooms
$\frac{1}{2}$ cup chicken broth (or stock)
3 tblsp balsamic vinegar
1 tblsp soy sauce
1 tblsp margarine or butter
2 tsp light brown sugar
4 pieces of boneless skinless salmon
$\frac{1}{4}$ tsp salt
$\frac{1}{8}$ tsp coarsely ground black pepper
12oz pre-washed spinach

Sutton

JOHN THORNBURN

COTSWOLD TROUT ON A COMPOTE OF ROASTED TOMATOES WITH RED ONION, BLACK OLIVE AND PESTO SAUCE

Race Consultant
Masterchef finalist

As a team manager for nearly four decades, John Thornburn worked with several talented drivers in their early careers, who went on to become World Champions: Denny Hulme, Jack Brabham, Keke Rosberg and Nigel Mansell. His major success came with Alan McKechnie's Formula 5000 team, winning the 1974 European Championship with British driver, Bob Evans.

Today, he manages Alex Portman in GTs and the team's Le Mans entry, also Rob Austin in Renault Sports. John's penchant and talent for cooking stems from his early years whilst travelling extensively in France with different teams; a talent he demonstrated on BBC's Masterchef.

At a BRDC/Masterchef Charity Lunch, held at Silverstone, as one of the three Masterchef contestants from the Midlands, he supervised Gilmour and Pethers' chefs as they prepared his recipe for Cotswold Trout as part of the menu. The lunch and charity auction raised £10,800 for the Gornji Vakuf Project (set up by the UN to help the war stricken children).

4 trout fillets each 200g (7oz)
120ml extra virgin olive oil
1 clove of garlic, chopped
juice of 1 lemon
30ml (2tblsp) white wine
50g (2oz) black olives, chopped
6 plum tomatoes
sea salt and freshly ground
black pepper
10ml (2tsp) oil
20g (1oz) basil leaves, chopped
12 coriander seeds
pinch of sugar

PESTO SAUCE
50g (2oz) basil leaves
150ml (1/4 pint) extra virgin olive oil
1 clove garlic
25g (1oz) pine nuts
20g (3/4 oz) Parmesan cheese,
freshly grated
sea salt and freshly ground
black pepper

To make the pesto sauce, put all the ingredients into a blender and work until smooth, set aside.

Heat the olive oil in a pan, add garlic and onion and fry gently for 3 minutes.

Add lemon juice, wine and olives and cook for 4 mins.

Dice 2 of the plum tomatoes and add to pan. Season with salt and pepper to taste, remove from heat and cool.

Halve the other 4 tomatoes and remove seeds. Place in a pan with the oil and cook on a high heat for 1 - 2 mins until lightly coloured.

Transfer to a shallow baking tray, sprinkle with shredded basil, coriander seeds, salt, pepper and sugar.

Spoon about a third of the onion and olive mixture into another baking tray and place the trout on top. Season with salt and pepper and spoon on the rest of the onion and olive mixture.

Place the tomatoes and trout in a preheated oven 230C/Gas mark 8 for 4 mins.

Arrange the tomatoes on warm plates and put the trout on top.

Add the pan juices from the tomatoes to the onion and olive mixture. Sprinkle this around the trout and drizzle with pesto sauce, then serve at once.

Family of motor racing addicts – 4 children, 3 granddaughters, 8 grandsons and 1 great grandson.
One of the Racey Recipe collaborators.
Cliff raced a Cooper MG – JOY500, Tojeiro Bristol – LOY500 and Lotus Eleven – NOY1. He competed in Monte Carlo and RAC Rallies, the latter once with the late David Blakeley. LOY500 starred in the film 'Dance with a Stranger'.

Back in the 60's we bought a lovely villa right on the beach in a little fishing village called Los Boliches in Spain. Together with my husband Cliff and four children, many happy holidays were spent there over the years. Sometimes the Hill, Leston and Taylor families stayed at a villa near ours, and, with eleven children between us, their villa was the place to go as they had a swimming pool. Even more so when Graham managed a visit between Grands Prix, and Jochen Rindt once dropped in – literally – he fell in the pool on top of my youngest daughter!

Having heard of the famous Tuesday Market which stretches for miles along the streets of adjoining Fuengirola, I volunteered to drive to the enormous fish market to get the shopping. Finding space in the shade to park Cliff's 1963 Cadillac Fleetwood Convertible was a nightmare, but eventually I deposited my large bag of fresh scallops on the floor in the back and browsed around the market stalls, losing all track of time, as one does. On returning to the car, not only had I got a parking ticket, but the scallop shells had opened and they had escaped out of the bag. My drive back to the villa broke all records as I listened to the spooky rustling of my slippery passengers!

SYLVIA DAVIS

COQUILLES SAINT JACQUES

Wife of the late Cliff Davis
Co-director/choreographer/lyricist of the Irwin/Davis Productions of the infamous Doghouse Cabarets and Pantomimes 1971 to 1991.

Preheat oven to 220C/425F/Gas Mark 7.

Remove fresh scallops from shells, discard greyish flesh and little black sac attached to each. Rinse and dry carefully.

Gently cook scallops in milk for 10 minutes. Drain and reserve milk.

In another saucepan melt butter and add flour. Mix well, cook for 2 to 3 minutes.

Remove from heat and gradually add milk.

Bring to the boil stirring until thickened.

Add half the cheese and seasoning, mix well and heat until melted.

Place the scallops in an ovenproof dish, pour sauce over them and cover with mashed potatoes and remaining grated cheese.

Cook in the oven for 10 minutes or place under the grill until golden brown.

This is a very filling family dish but can be served more elegantly, au gratin, on well scrubbed and dried scallop shells. Cook as above. Place scallops, whole or chopped on each shell, spoon over sauce, sprinkle with breadcrumbs and grated cheese and grill until lightly browned.

Serves 6

18 fresh scallops
1 pint of milk
2oz (60g) butter
2oz (60g) plain flour
2oz (60g) grated cheese
1 lb cooked potatoes, seasoned and mashed with a knob of butter

UH-OH! THE PRESS ARE COMING TO DINNER ...AGAIN!

If you are a team owner, the trick is not to take the media to a fancy restaurant. Far better to do your entertaining at the motor home in the paddock. That way, you save the embarrassment of trooping into a posh downtown establishment with what appears to be a tribe of pastoral nomads picked up on the way from the airport.

By issuing an invitation to dinner, the team in question is actually doing the flea-bitten freelance a favour by saving him the cost of a Big Mac or whatever delicacy he had in mind. Similarly, the offer of an early-evening meal in the paddock gives the thread-bare journo' the chance to say that pressure of time prevents him from returning to the hotel to change into a suit which doesn't actually exist.

It's a wonderful truth for members of the press that the standard of on-circuit catering is so high that it knocks all but the very best local hostelry into a cocked hat. And the advantage of home territory for the host goes beyond having to pay exorbitant restaurant bills which have been hit by that annual ripoff, the 'Add another 20% -The Grand Prix's in Town' surtax. This way, you control the finance, the food and, more important, the booze. In other words, you can have more of the latter.

It may come as a surprise to learn that journalists have been known to take the odd drink. It's often a chore, purely, you understand, to please the host. The things we have to do in order to maintain harmony in the paddock.. Actually, that's an unfortunate choice of phrase since harmony is the last word which springs to mind when the brandy appears and the hacks start singing. Some even go to the trouble of carrying a guitar all the way from home and then producing it with a flourish and a surprised look which suggests they have just found the musical instrument tucked in their back pocket.

The fact is, they treat the guitars with greater care than their lap top computers. Doesn't make sense really. If you think we can't write, you should hear us sing. But at least by holding the soiree in the middle of a semi-deserted paddock, a local restaurateur has been saved the embarrassment of having his regulars scared off and his entertainment licence revoked for contravening the Trade Descriptions Act. We media people are thoughtful like that when it comes to relieving a wealthy team of a square meal and a glass of something nice.

FAVOURITE RESTAURANTS

DEREK and MISTI BELL
Favourite restaurant at Le Mans. La Chatte sur le Tois. The Hotel de France, Le Mans.

TONY BROOKS
Drove for BRM, Vanwall, Ferrari, Yeoman Credit Racing

Tony and Pina's favourite restaurant is EL BURINOT at PERATALLADA, a beautiful medieval
Spanish village a few miles inland from an unspoilt part of the COSTA BRAVA, SPAIN.
Skilfully converted stables provide a series of intimate dining rooms for the family run restaurant and
we are always guaranteed a warm welcome.

A favourite menu would be:

Large slices of local toasted bread dipped in olive oil and grated with tomato.

A selection of local sausages and salami.

Lamb chops charcoal grilled with chips fried in olive oil.

Crèma Catalana - to call it a type of custard fails to convey it's light, delicate unique flavour.

What really puts the finishing touches to a fine meal in a wonderfully relaxing, rustic atmosphere is
the local, chilled, unadulterated red wine which, providing you have a strong willed volunteer driver
in the party, can be drunk in large quantities without any regrets the following morning.
We've had many parties at El Burinot, the individual dining areas avoiding any embarrassment as the
wine sweeps away the inhibitions to the point where, one year a member of our party did a
Frank Sinatra impression which seemed like the real thing – well almost !

SHINJI NAKANO
Shinji adores having his meals at the CAVALLINO HOTEL, where he lives when visiting the
MINARDI factory at FAENZA, ITALY. The hotel's restaurant is well known for it's typical Italian dishes.

MEAT EATERS

Baron Emmanuel de Graffenried raced for Maserati from 1950-1956,
"We used to eat red meat and drink red wine before a race, we thought it made us strong. I enjoyed steak medium rare and pommes frites."

Estaban Tuero Formula 1 driver Minardi ('98). He loves Assado, which as far as we can gather, is meat roasted on a spit over an open fire and a great Argentine speciality.

Goncarlo Gomes GT Chrysler Viper driver ('98). He likes a medium steak with a fried egg served with french fries.

Luciano Burti. Formula 3 driver ('98/'99). He prefers his Brazilian Beef well done.

Jamie Davis Formula 3000 ('98/'99). Jamie said that his favourite meal is the 'Full Sunday Monty,' Roast Beef Sunday lunch with all the trimmings, as made by his mother.

Jools Holland Musician and Formula 1 fan, is another Sunday lunch fan 'as cooked by his Nan'.

Joe Saward. Journalist: "I had dinner with ALAIN PROST in a Churrascaria in Sao Paulo when he had just become a team owner and I was amazed at the vast amount of red meat he was shovelling into his mouth. He had a manic look on his face and kept repeating: "I love meat, I love meat. They never let me eat it when I was a driver.""

Tarte au Citron
John Thornburn

Fatal Chocolate Thingy
Georgie Shaw

Sticky Toffee Pudding
Damon Hill

Caramalised Carrots
John Thornburn

Spicey Potatoes
Howden Ganley

Cabbage with Sesame Seeds
John Thornburn

Ginger and Orange Marinated Lamb
Mike and Anne Kimpton

Tuna or Salmon Mousse
Stirling and Susie Moss

meat

Sporting Pictures (UK)

BERNIE AND SLAVICA ECCLESTONE

CHICKEN PRIMOSTEN STYLE

Bernie Ecclestone, Chief Executive Officer, Formula One Administration Ltd
Vice-President, Fédération Internationale de l'Automobile, Promotional Affairs

Bernie Ecclestone, the Tzar of Grand Prix motor racing, began his racing career as a motor-cycle rider and successful driver (Cooper, Connaught); then as team owner of Brabham which won two world championships. He sold the team to concentrate on business and moved into administration and promotion of the sport representing all the Formula 1 teams. A visionary with legendary negotiating skills, Bernie has developed Grand Prix racing and the FIA Formula 1 World Championship into one of the world's greatest sporting spectacles, watched by a global audience, thanks to television, that can be counted in billions.

3lb (1.2kg) chicken
Ioz (30g) flour
5tbsp oil
2oz (60g) Parma ham, Prosciutto or smoked bacon
5oz (150g) onion
6 small fresh tomatoes or
2 tablespoons tomato purée
3 cloves garlic
1tbsp Vegeta
2fl oz (50ml) Sherry or Prosecco
2 tblsp capers
18oz (500g) peas
18oz (500g) new potatoes
salt and pepper
parsley

Wash the chicken and cut into pieces. Sprinkle with salt and flour, fry in hot oil until brown on all sides. Remove from pan.

In the same oil, briefly fry the cubed prosciutto/parma ham/bacon and the chopped onion.

Add the peeled and diced tomatoes, chopped garlic and then add the chicken pieces.

Sprinkle with Vegeta, pour in the sherry diluted with a little water.

Add the capers and peas and continue cooking until the meat is tender.

Add a little water, if necessary.

When the meat is almost cooked, add the cubed potatoes and the pepper.

Finally garnish with chopped parsley leaves.

Sutton

Double Formula 1 World Champion 1994, 1995, Benetton
1987 European and German Kart Champion
1988 Formula Konig, German Champion
1990 German Formula 3 Championship (5 wins)
1990 Won the prestigious Macau and Fuji Formula 3 races
1990-1991 Won Mexico City, Autopolis WSP races (member of Mercedes junior team).
1991-1999 Formula 1 Driver: Jordan, Benetton, Ferrari
Grand Prix Wins: 33

Since he burst onto the Formula 1 scene, qualifying seventh for Jordan at the 1991 Belgian Grand Prix, Michael Schumacher has emerged as 'the man to beat' and named the 'Rainmaster' for his awesome performances in the wet. His assertive and exciting driving style allows Michael to sythe his Ferrari through traffic like a hot knife through butter! Today, he carries the hopes and prayers of Ferrari and the whole of Italy on his mission to win the Formula 1 World Championship for the most famous marque in Grand Prix racing.

Could the secret of his famous podium leap be something to do with these dumplings.......

KNUCKLE OF VEAL

Trim off the fat and make slits in the meat which you fill with the garlic.

Season well with salt and pepper.

Pre-heat the oven to 280C.

Place meat in heavy casserole and cook for ½ hour

Pour in 1½ pints/1 litre of stock.

Return to the oven, reduce heat to 200C cover and cook for 2½ hours.

Remove meat, skim off fat and make a gravy from the juices.

MICHAEL & CORINNA SCHUMACHER

KNUCKLE OF VEAL WITH DUMPLINGS AND RED CABBAGE

Formula 1 Driver Scuderia Ferrari

Mazzi/Sutton

BAVARIAN DUMPLINGS

Put the stock on to boil.

Put the bread in a bowl and moisten with a little stock.

Melt the butter and fry the onion and parsley and reserve in another bowl. Fry the breadcrumbs and drain on kitchen paper. Beat the eggs together and mix all the ingredients together except breadcrumbs.

Form mixture into moderate sized balls, drop into boiling stock and simmer for 15 minutes.

Before serving sprinkle with breadcrumbs.

Note. Before forming all the mixture into balls it is advisable to test one in the boiling stock. If it crumbles, a little flour should be added to the mixture.

BAVARIAN CABBAGE

Wash and quarter the cabbage and shred it finely lengthwise.

Chop the onion finely. Chop the apple.

Melt the butter in a thick saucepan and fry the onion lightly.

Add the cabbage, chopped apple, salt, pepper, sugar, stock and caraway seeds.

Cover the pan tightly and simmer very gently for 1 hour.

Sprinkle in the flour and stir. Add wine, stir and bring to the boil.

Serves 6
1 large knuckle of veal
or 680g/1½ lbs lean stewing veal
home made stock or a stock cube
garlic

BAYRISCHE KNODEL - BAVARIAN DUMPLINGS
1½ litre/2 pints of stock
3 eggs
4 oz (120g) stale bread
1oz (30g) breadcrumbs
nutmeg
2oz (60g) butter
salt and pepper
1 tsp dried mixed herbs
A little chopped onion and parsley

BAYRISCHES KRAUT - BAVARIAN CABBAGE
1 large red cabbage
1 desertspoon sugar
1 onion
¼ pint stock or water
1 cooking apple
a few caraway seeds
3oz (90g) butter
1 tblsp flour
salt and pepper
⅛ pint white wine or vinegar

Sutton

RON AND LISA DENNIS

CHICKEN PARMESAN WITH BASIL

Ron Dennis, Group Managing Director, McLaren International

4 large chicken fillets
1 cup fresh breadcrumbs
1/3 cup grated Parmesan cheese
1 tblsp chopped parsley
3 rashers bacon
3oz (90g) butter
2 cloves garlic
1 tsp Worcestershire sauce
1/2 tsp dry mustard

BASIL SAUCE.
1/3 cup oil
1/4 cup white vinegar
1 clove garlic
1 cup fresh basil leaves
1/3 cup cream
1 egg yolk
salt and pepper

Combine in a bowl, breadcrumbs, cheese and parsley.

Chop bacon finely and fry in a pan until crisp. Drain. Add bacon to breadcrumb mixture.

Melt butter in a saucepan, add crushed garlic, Worcestershire sauce, and dry mustard. Mix well.

Dip chicken fillets in butter mixture and place in shallow ovenproof dish.

Press crumb mixture on top of each fillet. Bake, uncovered in a moderate oven for 20 to 25 minutes.

Serve with basil sauce.

Basil Sauce. Combine in saucepan, oil, vinegar, crushed garlic, finely chopped fresh basil leaves and cream, stir until heated through.

Add egg yolk and stir until sauce thickens. Do not boil. Season with salt and pepper.

Sporting Pictures (UK)

McLaren International headed by Ron Dennis has become one of the most successful Formula 1 teams in the history of Grand Prix racing, with seven constructors' championships and eight drivers' titles to add to Team McLaren's previous victories. In addition to the current world championship winning Formula 1 team, McLaren Cars won the 1995 Le Mans 24 Hours at their first attempt, whilst the road version recently entered the record books with a world-beating time for supercars. McLaren's latest innovation, the twin-seater Formula 1 car, has to be the ultimate marketing and promotional vehicle. A self-confessed enthusiast at heart, the McLaren boss readily swops his office seat for the hot seat and a blast up the famous Goodwood Hill during the annual Festival of Speed.

PADDOCK DRESSAGE

Ron and I were always having daft bets, and on one occasion he was complaining about the Press dressing in a slovenly fashion at race tracks. I replied that what could one expect, when the wine being served was so dreadful.

'If you supply Chateau Petrus, I will come in a dinner jacket.'

We agreed that we had a bet and so in Budapest in mid-August, I turned up at the race track in a full DJ and Ron duly produced a bottle of Petrus which we drank together - and very nice it was too....

JOE SAWARD Journalist

1987 Finnish Formula 3 Champion
1988 GM Euroseries Champion
1990 British Formula 3 Champion, West Surrey Racing
1991-1999 Formula 1 Driver: Lotus, McLaren
Grand Prix wins: 9 (end of '98)

The Flying Finn was a highly popular Formula 1 World Champion in 1998. Mr. SuperCool produced some stunning drives to clinch the title, most notably, Monaco, the Nurburgring and Suzuka.

MIKA AND ERJA HAKKINEN

MIKA'S SPECIAL HOMEMADE SAUSAGE WITH ONION GRAVY

Mika Hakkinen 1998 FIA Formula 1 World Champion, McLaren

His sister Nina says that this is one of his Favourite recipes.

Brown the onion rings in a pan.

Melt the butter or oil in a saucepan and stir in the flour until smooth.

Slowly add the water, meat stock cube and allspice.

Pour into the pan with the onions, cover and simmer for 30 minutes.

Strain the onions, add the sausage cubes, stir for 10 minutes.

Add the cream or French cream, add salt to taste.

3 tblsp butter or oil
5 tblsp white flour
2-3 cups of water
1 meat stock cube
½ HK blue sausage
1 onion
single cream or French cream to taste
salt and allspice

Sporting Pictures (UK)

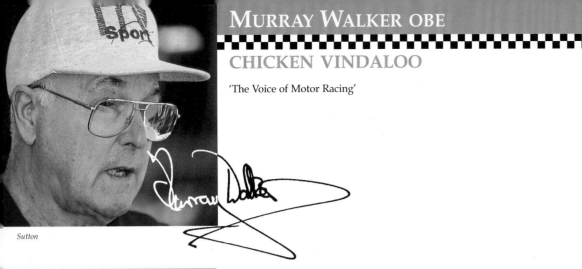

Sutton

MURRAY WALKER OBE

CHICKEN VINDALOO

'The Voice of Motor Racing'

Murray Walker recently celebrated an incredible 50 years of radio and television commentary for the BBC. Renowned throughout the world for his boundless enthusiasm, passion and in-depth knowledge of Grand Prix motor racing. Murray's voice is as familiar and welcome as the scream from the current Formula 1 engines, and even delivered at similar decibels.

It's all GO! GO! GO! As the five pairs of red lights go out and Murray Walker, heads ITV's Grand Prix commentary team into the 21st century.

His choice of dish, is as hot and spicy as some of his commentaries.

Vindaloos can be made from lamb, beef or prawns but Murray's favourite is made with chicken. It is very hot! However, you can control the heat by putting in just as many red chillies as you think you can manage.

Serves 6-8

2 tsp whole cumin seeds
3-4 dried red chillies
1 tsp black peppercorns
1 tsp cardamom seeds
a 3 inch stick of cinnamon
1 1/2 tsp whole black mustard seeds
1 tsp whole fenugreek seeds
5 tblsp white wine vinegar
1 1/2 tsp salt
1 tsp light brown sugar
10 tblsp vegetable oil
6-8 oz onions, peeled and sliced into fine half rings
4-6 tblsp plus 8fl oz water
6-8 portions of chicken
a 1 inch cube of fresh ginger, peeled and grated
a small whole bulb of garlic, with all the cloves peeled
1 tblsp ground coriander seeds
1/2 tsp ground turmeric

Grind the cumin, chillies, peppercorns, cardamom seeds, cinnamon, black mustard seeds and fenugreek in a coffee or spice grinder. Place the ground spices in a bowl and add the vinegar, salt and sugar and mix.

Heat the oil in a wide, heavy pot over a medium heat and fry the onions until they are brown and crisp.

Remove them with a slotted spoon and put them in a food processor or blender.

Add 2-3 tblsp of water and purée. Add this purée to the ground spices and you have your vindaloo paste!

This may be made in advance or if you think this sounds too much like hard work, you could use some Patak's Vindaloo Paste according to the instructions!

Dry the chicken pieces.

Put the ginger and garlic into the blender or processor, add 2-3 tblsp of water and blend to a smooth paste.

Heat the remaining oil in a large, heavy pan, over a medium heat and brown the chicken on all sides. Remove and keep warm.

Put the ginger paste in the pan and turn down the heat a little.

Stir the paste for a few seconds and add the coriander and turmeric.

Stir a little more and then add the chicken.

Stir in the vindaloo paste and 8 fl oz of water.

Cover and simmer gently for about an hour until the chicken is thoroughly cooked, stirring occasionally.

Serve with plenty of boiled rice and eat with extreme caution!

Bernie Ecclestone, the Tzar of Grand Prix motor racing, began his racing career as a motor-cycle rider and successful driver (Cooper, Connaught); then as team owner of Brabham which won two world championships. He sold the team to concentrate on business and moved into administration and promotion of the sport representing all the Formula 1 teams. A visionary with legendary negotiating skills, Bernie has developed Grand Prix racing and the FIA Formula 1 World Championship into one of the world's greatest sporting spectacles, watched by a global audience, thanks to television, that can be counted in billions.

FISH ON FRIDAY

Last year at Spa, we went out to dinner with Bernie, at some ludicrously expensive place.
Bernie does not seem to care about food, as he was heard to mutter that the artistic mouthfuls of creative cuisine which turned up every half an hour reminded him of his childhood.
"We always used to have fish with strawberry jam every Friday night" he muttered, as we devoured the curious mixture set before us. "I think I'd settle for some chicken nuggets."

By JOE SAWARD Journalist

BERNIE AND SLAVICA ECCLESTONE

DUCK WITH MLINCI

Bernie Ecclestone, Chief Executive Officer, Formula One Administration Ltd
Vice-President, Fédération Internationale de l'Automobile, Promotional Affairs

Sporting Pictures (UK)

Wash the duck and rub it with salt and Vegata inside and out.

Allow to rest for several hours or overnight.

Preheat oven to 180C/350F/Gas mark 4

Before roasting, spread lard over the duck.

Place in roasting tin, add a little water and roast slowly, basting it in it's own juices.

When the duck is done, remove from the pan and keep warm.

Remove the surplus fat from the roasting juices.

Place Mlinci into the tin, mix and bake briefly.

Carve the duck and arrange with the Mlinci on a large plate.

Garnish with parsley and serve.

Serves 6

1 Duck about 2kg (4$^{1}/_{2}$lbs)
1 tblsp Vegata
lard
salt

MLINCI
12oz (350g) flour
salt and water

PROF. SID WATKINS

NIGERIAN CURRY

Sporting Pictures (UK)

FIA Medical Delegate, Consultant neuro-surgeon,
President of the FIA Expert Advisory Group

Prof. Sid was cornered by Georgie at Silverstone and gave her this recipe which isn't exactly a recipe as such but is more a philosophy for making the best of what is to hand. This could be the result of growing up in Liverpool where the staple food is 'Scouse' a cross between Lancashire hot pot and Irish stew. The Prof described it as a stew of neck of lamb with potatoes, parsnips, turnips and (he added with a twinkle in his eye and a wry smile) anything left over that was lying around the kitchen, even the cat! Although his favourite food, he admitted, was well done Aberdeen Angus steak with chips, he reminisced about the curries he enjoyed out in the Nigerian bush, while in the army and finishing the story he added: "Although I didn't catch the maleria bug, the only one I caught in Nigeria was a life-long motor racing bug!" Here is The Prof's hot, spicy and fruity recipe for Nigerian Curry.

For nearly twenty years Professor Sid Watkins has attended just about every round of the Formula 1 world championship in his role as Medical Supremo, in charge of circuit medical facilities and personnel. 'The Prof' as he is universally known, is one of the world's most distinguished neuro-surgeons and a passionate motor racing fan, a passion which dates back to the mid-fifties when he rallied in Nigeria whilst serving in the British Army. Under his supervision safety standards have improved dramatically, with ultra modern fully equipped medical centres replacing previously outdated and inadequate facilities. Added to his work on the FIA Safety Commission and Expert Advisory Group, The Prof has helped minimalise the risks to present day Grand Prix drivers. A great character who enjoys a good cigar.

Dissect a chicken or guinea fowl and place in a large heavy pan.

Cover with a layer of fresh (or tinned) tomatoes and sliced yams.

Season to taste with salt, pepper and curry powder.

Cook over a low flame for several hours, adding liquid to keep the meat covered.

Towards the end of the cooking time add sliced bananas, paw paw, lemon, grapefruit and orange slices, and peanuts (with the proviso that if one is allergic to peanuts this should be omitted as sudden death will occur).

Season with cayenne pepper, serve with boiled rice and side dishes of sliced cucumber, sliced tomatoes, grated fresh coconut, sliced bananas and lime pickle.

The meal should cause the ingester to break out in a heavy perspiration which cools the skin which is a great aid to tolerating the climate in which the meal is eaten; in the bush without air conditioning or fans etc.

DREAMER

Ron Dennis has a lively taste for alcoholic substances – usually in league with Prof. Sid Watkins. I remember one evening in the Log Cabin bar in Suzuka, Ron bet me that I would not drink a very large glass full of whisky. I agreed to do so in exchange for some exclusive news stories (or something equally silly) but before I did so, I decided it was wise to ask 'The Prof' if I would die as a result of this. He said: "Don't worry old boy, lie on the floor and I will give you a lobotomy with the knife and fork I happen to have here. You will have a lovely time for about twenty minutes and then you won't remember a thing." He was absolutely right.

JOE SAWARD Journalist

OZ RACK OF LAMB

1955 – 1970 Formula 1 Driver: Cooper, Maserati, Lotus, Brabham

Triple Formula 1 World Champion, 1955, 1960, *1966

*The only driver to win a Formula 1 World Championship in a car bearing his own name, Brabham Repco.

Grand Prix wins: 14

Constructor: 1964 Founded Brabham Racing Organisation.

First win with Dan Gurney, at the French Grand Prix.

David Hayhoe

Trim away some of the excess fat from the top of the lamb, leaving only a thin layer.

Heat a heavy based frying pan. Place the lamb fat-side down in the pan over a high heat and cook until the outside of the fat is brown.

Neither moisture or fat is needed in the pan as sufficient will come from the meat as it begins to brown.

Discard all the fat from the pan. There is no need to wash it but wipe it with a paper towel.

Mix the port, stock, bay leaf, sultanas and garlic together.

Depending on the saltiness of the stock, season the mixture with salt and pepper.

Pour over the lamb and allow to marinate until ready to cook.

Cook in the pan for between 15 and 20 minutes until the meat is cooked to the desired taste.

Mix the cornflour with some water, add the liquid from the lamb and cook until the sauce has thickened.

Serve the lamb accompanied by the sauce.

Serves 4
2 racks of lamb, each consisting of about 6 chops
salt and pepper
1 cup of port
$\frac{1}{2}$ cup of chicken stock
1 bay leaf
3 tablespoons sultanas
2 whole cloves of garlic
2 teaspoons cornflour

ROCCO BENETTON

CARPACCIO CON FORMAGGIO GRANA

Chief Executive, Benetton Formula 1

The youngest Chief Executive of any Formula 1 team in the pitlane, twenty nine year old Rocco Benetton first joined Benetton Formula as Commercial Director in 1997. Rocco finished his education in America, gaining an Engineering Degree at Boston University; he entered the business community with the Oppenheimer bank, then Alpha Investment Management, rising from consultant to Managing Director. In just two years of his appointment the company was managing a 1.5 billion dollar capital and nearly 300 million dollars in investment venture capital.

The youngest son of Luciano Benetton, Rocco gives us a taste for his passion for Italy and food with his favourite meal.

12oz (350g) beef fillet
2 tblsp lemon juice
4 tblsp best olive oil
Salt and fresh ground black pepper
A piece of Parmesan cheese
Rocket leaves to garnish

Rocco Benetton's favourite meal consists of:
Insalata di Rucola
(Rocket Salad)
Pasta con Mozzarella, Pomodoro e Basilico
(Pasta with Mozzarella, Tomato and Basil)
Carpaccio con formaggio Grana
(Sliced Beef with Parmesan cheese)
Crosta di Mele
(Apple Tart)
Caffe
(Coffee)

To make the beef easier to slice thinly, it is best to chill it thoroughly.

Slice it as thinly as possible with a very sharp knife.
Place a small pile of beef slices on serving plates, this amount should feed four.

Mix the olive oil and lemon juice and season with salt and pepper.
Drizzle this over the meat.

Garnish with the rocket leaves and then sprinkle very thin shavings of Parmesan cheese over the top.

ALAIN PROST

Prost GP

POULET BASQUAISE

Team Principal Prost Grand Prix
4 times Formula 1 World Champion 1985, 1986, 1989, 1993

*1980-1993 Formula 1 Driver: McLaren,
Renault, Ferrari, Williams
Grand Prix wins: 51
Owner of Prost Grand Prix*

Since hanging up his helmet and closing the record books on his hugely successful racing career, Alain was appointed as special Ambassador to the Renault Group until 1995, he moved to McLaren as Special Consultant and Adviser before purchasing the former Ligier Formula 1 team in 1997 (renamed, Prost Grand Prix). 1998 Prost Grand Prix relocated from Magny-Cours to a new purpose built facility outside Paris. Alain retains his two drivers for the 1999 season - Olivier Panis and Jarno Trulli.

Cut the chicken into pieces. Heat 2 tblsp olive oil in a pan, add the chicken pieces and brown over a moderate heat.

Remove chicken from pan and put into a flameproof casserole.

Add the white wine and bouquet garni, season with salt and pepper.

Cover and cook in a moderate oven for 1½ hours.

Cut the peppers in half and core, seed and de-stalk. Put them under a hot grill until the skins are charred. Remove from grill and put the peppers in an airtight container or plastic bag (sealed). Leave to cool for 10 minutes.

Peel the tomatoes, remove the seeds and chop coarsely.

Peel and thinly slice the onions.

Remove the skins from the peppers. Cut the flesh into strips.

Heat the rest of the olive oil in the frying pan, add the onions and cook until soft.

Add the peppers and cook for 10 minutes, add the tomatoes and season to taste.

Cook over a low heat until the ingredients are soft.

About 20 minutes before the chicken has finished cooking add the contents of the frying pan to the casserole. Continue to simmer gently until the end of the cooking time.

3lb (1.5kg) chicken
4 tblsp olive oil
¼ pint dry white wine
1 bouquet garni
salt and pepper
2 large green peppers
2 large sweet red peppers
4 medium sized tomatoes
6 medium sized onions

Sutton

BREAST OF HEREFORDSHIRE WOOD PIGEON WITH CHINESE SPICES

Race Consultant
Masterchef finalist

Remove the breasts from pigeons, rub with Chinese spice mixture and set aside.

Chop up carcasses, heat oil in a heavy pan, add pigeon bones and brown over a moderate heat. Add shallots, garlic, ginger and mushrooms, sauté until lightly browned.

Add thyme and tomatoes and cook for 2 mins.

Add vinegar and cook until almost evaporated.

Add wine and let bubble until reduced by half.

Add honey, soy sauce and 400ml (14 fl oz) water. Simmer for about 1½ hours until reduced by half.

Strain through a fine sieve into a clean pan, reheat, whisking in the butter a little at a time.

To cook pigeon, heat oil in a heavy frying pan, add pigeon breasts and cook over high heat for 4 minutes. Turn and cook other side for 2 mins.

Transfer to warmed plates and serve with :

Fried new potatoes with spring onions

Caramelised Carrots

Cabbage with sesame seeds.

CHINESE SPICE MIXTURE

Mix equal quantities of grated galangal, star anise, cloves, ground ginger, ground cinnamon, ground nutmeg, celery, salt, ground coriander, allspice, dried black beans and dried orange peel. Grind to a powder and store in an airtight jar to be used as needed.

---

4 wood pigeons
30ml (2tsp) oil
Chinese spice mixture

SAUCE
pigeon carcasses
15ml (1tsp) oil
60g (2oz) shallots, chopped
3 cloves of garlic, chopped
15g (¹/₂ oz) root ginger, chopped
1 thyme sprig
2 tomatoes, chopped
60g (2oz) mushrooms, chopped
60ml (4 tblsp) red wine vinegar
15g (¹/₂ oz) honey
5 ml (1 tsp) soy sauce
30g (1oz) butter

VEGETABLE ACCOMPANIMENTS FOR BREAST OF WOOD PIGEON

FRIED NEW POTATOES WITH SPRING ONIONS
8 new potatoes, salt
60ml (1oz) oil, 30g (1oz) butter
8 spring onions chopped

Cook the potatoes in their skins until almost tender, drain and slice.
Heat the oil and butter in a pan and add the potatoes, cook turning until golden.
Season with salt and pepper and add the spring onions.
Cook for 1 minute, drain on kitchen paper and serve.

CARAMELISED CARROTS
4 carrots, salt
15g (¹/₂ oz) fresh root ginger, shredded
30g (1oz) butter, 20g (4 tsp) sugar

Slice the carrots on the diagonal. Add to pan of boiling water with half the ginger.
Bring to the boil, lower heat and simmer for 4 mins until just cooked.
Drain and let cool.
Melt butter in pan, add the sugar and a splash of water. Heat until the butter is dissolved then add carrots and remaining ginger.
Cook until the carrots are tender and lightly coloured.

CABBAGE WITH SESAME SEEDS
200g (7oz) cabbage, cored
salt and freshly ground black pepper
30g (1oz) butter, 20ml (4tsp) sesame oil
5ml (1tsp) sesame seeds, toasted

Cut cabbage into squares and cook for 4 minutes, drain and refresh under cold water.
Heat butter in frying pan with sesame oil.
Add cabbage season with salt and pepper and toss until warmed through.
Arrange on warmed side plates and sprinkle with toasted sesame seeds.

PORK FILLET WITH PORT

The only driver to win two consecutive world titles the Formula 1 World Championship ('92) and the Indy World Series title ('93).

Rose/Sutton

1980 – 1992 Formula 1 Driver: Lotus, Williams, Ferrari, McLaren
1992 Formula 1 World Champion, Williams
1993 –1994 Indy Car Driver: Newman-Haas
1993 Indy Car Champion, Newman-Haas, Lola
1994 –1995 Formula 1 Driver: Williams, McLaren
Grand Prix wins: 31

One of our most exciting Grand Prix drivers whose gutsy driving style fired the nations' imagination like no other. Mansell made the impossible over taking manoeuvre possible, even outgunning the legendary Ayrton Senna on occasion. When on a charge, Mansell was pure magic, breathtaking to watch. He roused the super cool Brits into the most passionate supporters of Red 5. Mansellmania was born.

Cut pork fillet into half inch slices.

Heat oil in saucepan, fry meat, brown lightly to seal.

Remove from pan, keep on one side.

Add onion, red currant jelly, tomato purée and soy sauce.

Fry gently over low heat for 2 minutes and stir in flour.

Remove from heat, gradually stir in the stock until smooth.

Return to heat, boil until sauce thickens.

Add port and season to taste (if using wine, boil for 10 minutes).

Return pork to sauce, cook over a low heat for 10 minutes or until thoroughly cooked through.

Serve with accompanying vegetables.

2lb pork fillet
2 tblsp oil
1 small onion, sliced
2 tblsp of redcurrant jelly
2 tblsp tomato purée
1 tblsp soy sauce
2 level tsp plain flour
$^3/_4$ pint of chicken stock
$^1/_4$ pint of port or red wine

DON AND JOANNE NAMAN

CHICKEN POT PIE

Don Naman, Executive Director, The International Motor Sports Hall of Fame, Talladega, Alabama, U.S.A.

CHICKEN POT PIE
1 whole chicken, cooked and boned
(or 1 large canned chicken)
5 hard boiled eggs, chopped
2 cans mixed vegetables, drained
2 cans cream of mushroom soup
1 can cream of celery soup
1 cup chicken broth

CRUST
1 cup milk
1 cup mayonnaise
1 cup self raising flour

Lightly grease a large baking dish and arrange the cooked chicken pieces evenly in the dish.

In a medium boiler combine next five ingredients (eggs, vegetables, both kinds of soup and broth).

Heat to a boil and pour over the chicken.

To make the crust, combine all ingredients in a quart jar, replace lid and shake well until well mixed.

Pour the crust over all – evenly.

Bake at 350F/180C/Gas mark 4 until crust is golden brown.

JOHN BINTCLIFFE AND SHARI ANDREWS

PURE INDULGENCE

John Bincliffe, Saloon Driver and Principal, Bintcliffe Sport

Twice a BTCC winner with the four-wheel-drive Audi in 1997, John Bintcliffe is now running his own saloon car team with some success. As a Yorkshireman born in Bridlington, John probably grew up on a diet of jellied eels and tripe!

PURE INDULGENCE
Serves 2
2 plump chicken breasts
1 packet of strong shallots
10 fl oz double cream
1 dstsp of lemon pepper
1 large courgette
1 large clove of garlic
Penne pasta
salt

Cook pasta in boiling salted water for approximately 10 minutes.

Cut the chicken breasts into cubes and lightly fry in virgin olive oil until brown (approximately 2-3 mins). Add coarsely chopped shallots and crushed garlic and lightly fry until golden brown (approximately 5 minutes).

Add chopped courgettes and cook for a further 5 minutes.
Add double cream and the lemon pepper.
Simmer until sauce has thickened.

Drain pasta and add the cream chicken sauce. Stir together and serve immediately with some grated Parmesan cheese.

Serve with a Lollo Rosso and tomato salad with balsamic vinegar and olive oil dressing and crushed herb and garlic bread.

JEAN TODT

SCALOPPA DI VITELLO ALLA MILANESE
VEAL ESCALOPE MILANESE

Team Sporting Director, Ferrari

Sutton

Prior to his present position, Jean headed the entire motor sport programme for Automobiles Peugeot (for twelve years); accomplished major successes in the World Rally Championship (2 Drivers' and 2 Constructors' titles); 4 Paris-Dakar victories; the World Sports Car Championship and Le Mans 24 Hours. Jean won a World Rally Championship title himself, as a co-driver.

DAKAR'D GOAT

The only meal I remember eating with Jean Todt, was on the Paris-Dakar Rally in Agadez. I remember it being a memorable meal for me, although I am not sure that Todt actually touched it. It was Roast Goat, cooked (and therefore seasoned) with kerosene and spiced with a little sand – as indeed all food is when you are on the Paris-Dakar. I remember it being very good, but I don't think 'the Todt' actually ate any because the Peugeot team always had a French chef along with them and they always ate very well. Not very adventurous, but obviously efficient, given the number of times they won the Paris-Dakar.

JOE SAWARD Journalist

Put veal escalopes between layers of cling film and beat with a rolling pin or similar to flatten.

Dust with flour and season. Dip in beaten egg and then coat with breadcrumbs.

Fry in butter until golden brown on both sides and cooked right through.

Place on kitchen paper to drain excess fat.

Serve, garnished with lemon wedges and parsley.

---

4 Veal Escalopes
plain flour
1 large egg, beaten
1$\frac{1}{2}$ cups fresh breadcrumbs
100g (4oz) unsalted butter
salt and freshly ground black pepper
lemon and parsley to garnish

DANNY SULLIVAN

VEAL PICCATA

1972-1976 Raced in the UK: Formula Ford, Formula 3, Formula 2
1977-1982 Raced in the USA: Formula Atlantic, CanAm, Indy Car
1983 Formula 1 Driver: Tyrrell
1984-1985 Indy Car Driver
1985 Won *Indy 500, Team Penske
1988 Won Indy Car World Series Title, Team Penske
1998 Won Formula 1 race – Goodwood Motor Circuit Revival Meeting, Cooper

**1 medallion of veal for each person
butter for frying
flour for coating
1 or 2 lemons for squeezing**

Take small medallions of veal and lay under wax paper, hammer with a wooden mallet until softened up.

Take the medallions and LIGHTLY flour.

Melt a small amount of butter in a frying pan over a low to medium flame.

Cook the veal to preferred taste, turning once.

About halfway through cooking squeeze the juice of one or two lemons (depending on quantity) over the veal.

You can also do this with chicken or fish. Danny likes this served with French beans and wild rice.

Danny took the chequered flag and Indy 500 title only after surviving a 360 degree spin in front of Mario Andretti, seconds after passing him. Miraculously both drivers avoided contact and Danny retook the lead with just 3 laps to go!

Commenting to Racey Recipes after his triumphant drive at Goodwood: "It was super fun!" he enthused. "Phil Hill and Dan Gurney came over to congratulate me after the race and said 'Now you can say you have won a Formula 1 race and not many people can say that' – that was so nice of them."

ALLAN McNISH

HAGGIS

1988 British Formula Vauxhall Champion
1998 Won Le Mans 24 Hours, Porsche
1999 Toyota GT-One Driver with ex-GP driver Thierry Boutsen and Ralf
Kelleners to contest 1999 Le Mans 24 Hours Classic

Being a good Scot, Allan's favourite meal is haggis. While this can be obtained from good butchers and some super markets at relevant times, Hogmanay and Burn's night, Allan says the best are to be found at his favourite butcher in Dumfries. If you absolutely must make your own, here is how to do it.

HAGGIS
1 sheep's paunch, liver, kidneys,
heart and lights
1 lb oatmeal
1 lb beef suet
2 large onions
salt and pepper
finely grated nutmeg
juice of a lemon
1$\frac{1}{2}$ pints of stock

Soak the paunch overnight in salted water. Turn inside out and wash thoroughly.

Chop the kidneys and liver, cover with cold water and simmer for 1$\frac{1}{2}$ hours.
After $\frac{3}{4}$ of an hour add chopped heart and lights.
Chop them all very finely and add to the oatmeal, finely chopped suet, finely chopped onions salt, pepper, lemon juice, stock and a little nutmeg.
Mix well and stuff into the paunch. Allow space for the oatmeal to swell.
Sew up the opening and simmer gently for about 2$\frac{1}{2}$ to 3 hours.
Prick occasionally to allow steam to escape otherwise the paunch may burst.

Serve with mashed potatoes and neeps (swede) and gravy if desired.
Garlic and herbs may be added but this is not authentic.

CRAIG AND BARBARA POLLOCK

MINCE AND TATTIES

Craig Pollock, Managing Director, British American Racing

Jacques Villeneuve's former P.E. teacher in Switzerland, Craig has managed Jacques' racing career a number of years, since when the young Canadian has won the Indy 500 title, the Champ Car World title and the Formula 1 World Championship. Craig heads the British American Racing team as Managing Director in his first season of Grand Prix Racing with the team's No. 1 driver, Jacques Villeneuve.

Sutton

MINCE AND TATTIES
Serves 4
1 large onion, finely chopped
2 large carrots, finely chopped
1 lb of ground beef (steak)
Bisto or gravy granules
water
1 large spoon of double cream (optional)

As the new 'boys on the block', Craig's favourite recipe is remarkably 'old school' - the Scottish staple.

In a large frying pan brown onions, carrots and beef until done.

Add brown gravy, (Bisto and water).

Leave to cook on a low heat for 20 minutes.

Just before serving add double cream (optional).

Serve with Tatties (homemade mashed potatoes).

Sutton

KEN AND NORAH TYRRELL

VEAL CASSEROLE

Founder of Tyrrell Racing Organisation

Norah and I married in 1943 and at that time Norah had difficulty in boiling an egg! Foreign travel whetted her appetite for good food.
I now live like a king.

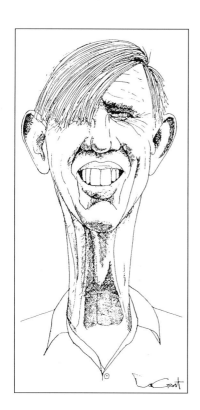

Get a good cut of veal, cut into pieces and shake in a bag of flour.

Cut up a few slices of lean bacon and saute with the veal in a little olive oil.

Add some white wine, parsley and herbs of choice and simmer for about $1\frac{1}{4}$ hours.

30 minutes before the end of cooking time add some mushrooms.

John Blunsden, Journalist

A former timber merchant, who took up motor racing as a hobby, discovered he wasn't as talented as some of his contemporaries and turned to team management, at which he quickly established himself as amongst the world's best. His talent-spotting prowess served him well, and Jackie Stewart repaid him by scoring all three of his World Championships as a Tyrrell team driver. Ken Tyrrell became a racing car constructor in his own right in 1970 when it was clear that buying off-the-shelf Formula One cars was no longer a recipe for success. Although lacking the immense financial resources of some rival teams, Team Tyrrell continued to make an impact in Grand Prix circles until 1998 when Ken sold the team to BAR.

GERHARD BERGER

THE BEST BERGER IN TOWN!

The secret of Gerhard Berger's carefree attitude is that he brought no emotional baggage with him when he arrived as a driver in F1. Grand Prix racing had not been part of the master plan; it had merely seemed like a good idea, something to do next. As a result, Berger was always his own man, finding no need for the entourage which most drivers seem to crave as a kind of crutch when in a public place. It would matter little to him if he had to eat on his own. One such occasion was in Budapest's Forum Hotel in August 1988.

A group of us asked if we could join him and that was to be the start of one of the most amusing evenings I can remember. As he regaled us with stories of his youth it was easy to understand why he is such a free spirit.

'When I was a kid, the snow was a big part of our lives,' he said. 'We used to get one boy to lie in the road and, when the car stopped, we would come up behind and hang on to the back bumper. The driver wouldn't know we were there; maybe five or six of us and the one at the exhaust would have a bad time! But we would go along at 50 mph with our feet in the snow. It was incredible! It was also dangerous. You would have to watch out for bridges and sewers, where the snow was melted. But you couldn't see it coming. We would always wear gloves and sometimes you would fall off and leave your gloves behind – still stuck to the bumper!'

As the courses came and went in the starched-linen splendour of the dining room, Gerhard moved on to his early racing career. It seemed he was not averse to shifting blame – and not too ashamed to tell us about it, as this story from his FF2000 days proved.

'It was in the support race for the German GP at Hockenheim. At the first corner, I went over someone's wheel. The car felt funny at the back but I was fourth, so I thought, keep going, this is okay.'

'Got to the chicane – no brakes! That's what had broken. Straight on, cars everywhere. An engine over there; a chassis here. I thought I had killed at least two people. They had to stop the race and there was hardly anyone left for the restart! Someone said it was his fault – pointing at another driver – and I said: 'Yes! It was him! He got the blame.....'

And so it went on. Don't ask me what was on the menu that night; I couldn't read it for laughing. You might say we had a Berger, very well done.

By MAURICE HAMILTON

Journalist. The Observer/BBC Radio 5 Live

WIENER SCHNITZEL

Motorsport Director, BMW
1984 – 1997 Formula 1 Driver: ATS, Arrows, Benetton, Ferrari, McLaren
Grand Prix wins: 12

One of the greatest characters in Formula 1, whose outrageous jokes and pranks with the likes of Ayrton Senna were legendary. However, the flamboyant play-boy image often played into his hands and the astute business trained Austrian was equally adept at skillfully negotiating his own contracts as trading fastest laps with the likes of Ayrton or winning from pole position as he did for Benetton at the 1997 German Grand Prix at Hockenheim, his last Grand Prix victory. In his present position as BMW's Motorsport Director, Gerhard is now totally committed to managing BMW's engine programme for WilliamsF1 in the year 2000.

Sutton

Wrap each fillet in cling film or similar and beat with rolling pin until thin.

Season and roll the fillets in the flour to coat thinly.

Beat the egg, dip the fillets into it and coat with breadcrumbs.

Heat the butter and oil in a heavy frying pan and when hot add the veal and fry each fillet until they are crisp and golden brown.

Drain on kitchen paper and serve garnished with sliced hard-boiled egg and lemon slices.

A BEANY-BERGER

Very few of the stories about Gerhard Berger involve food, as I think the subject was of very little interest to him, unless, the food in question, was spread over a naked lady – in which case, he would have been more attentive. I do remember dining in a godforsaken place in the middle of nowhere in Sweden and having a green bean land on my shoulder. I looked at it, looked around the restaurant and saw no-one at all (it was a lively place) so I said "Thank you Gerhard !"

He was rather taken aback that I knew he was there, because he was hidden around a corner. 'How did I know it was him?' He asked. I replied that no-one except a racing driver eats green beans if they have a choice of something else, and most of the other drivers were too reserved (without alcohol) to throw them around the restaurant. So it had to be him.....

JOE SAWARD Journalist

Fillet of veal slices ¹/₂ inch thick
Salt and freshly ground black pepper
1 egg
Breadcrumbs
Butter and vegetable oil mixture for frying
A little flour
I hard-boiled egg (for garnish)
1 lemon (for garnish)

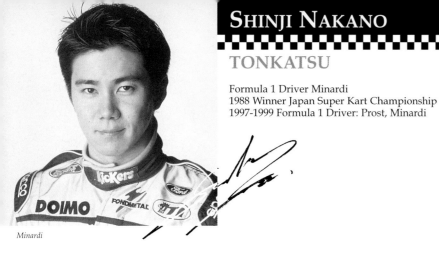

Minardi

SHINJI NAKANO

TONKATSU

Formula 1 Driver Minardi
1988 Winner Japan Super Kart Championship
1997-1999 Formula 1 Driver: Prost, Minardi

4 slices pork shoulder roast
(about 1cm thick)
4 tblsp of Mirin or dry Sherry
4 tblsp of soy sauce
a little garlic (crushed)
a little flour
1 egg (beaten)
1 cup soft white breadcrumbs
oil for shallow frying

Trim the excess fat off the meat and cut the border line between the meat and the fat in three or four places.

Marinate the meat in a mixture of soy sauce, Mirin or dry Sherry, garlic and pepper for 30 minutes.

Sprinkle flour on both sides and shake off any excess. Dip into the egg and then into the breadcrumbs, pressing them on firmly.

Chill for 1 hour or longer.

Heat oil to medium heat (about 180) in a large frying pan and fry, turning the slices over until both sides are golden brown.

Place on kitchen paper to absorb any excess oil, cut into slices and serve with raw shredded cabbage with mustard or tonkatsu sauce*.

Raw shredded cabbage is usually served with tonkatsu as it is thought to break down the fat in the tonkatsu.

*Although there are many recipes, tonkatsu sauce can be made easily by mixing Worcestershire sauce with tomato ketchup.

トンカツ

四人前。

材料。
豚肩ロース　4枚　（厚さやく1cm）。
ミリンまたはドライ・シェリー大さじ　4。
しょうゆ大さじ　4。
にんにくのすりおろし少々。
小麦粉少々。
溶き卵　一個分。
パン粉　コップ一杯。
揚げ油。

余分についている脂身を切り取り、肉と脂の境の筋を3－4ヶ所筋切りする。
30分ほどしょうゆ、ミリン（ドライ・シェリー）、にんにくとこしょうのたれにつける。
小麦粉を両面にまぶしつけ、余分な粉を落してから卵につけパン粉をしっかりつける。
一時間冷やす。
大きめのフライ・パンに揚げ油を中温に熱し（やく180°）、両面がキツネ色になるまで表裏を返しながら揚げる。
キッチン・タオルに乗せ、余分な油をすいとる。

1985 Won Formula Ford Festival
1987 British Formula 3 Champion (EJR)
1989 – 1999 Formula 1 Driver: Benetton, Tyrrell, Lotus, Sauber, Stewart
1989 Debut race finished 4th Brazilian Grand Prix, Benetton; just months after smashing both feet, the result of his accident at Brands Hatch (Jordan F3000).
1991 Won Le Mans 24 Hours, Mazda
Grand Prix wins: 2

JOHNNY HERBERT

ROAST BEEF, YORKSHIRE PUDDING, ROAST POTATOES

Formula 1 Driver Stewart

Sporting Pictures (UK)

Johnny's carefree demeanour hides a steely resolve and his desire to win. Perhaps Stewart and Ford can give him that opportunity in 1999. Forget your pasta, Johnny told Racey Recipes, that his favourite meal is Sunday lunch, with all the trimmings.

Pre heat the oven to 245C/475F/Gas mark 9

Rub the beef with a mixture of flour, salt and pepper and dry mustard.

Place on a roasting tin in the oven.

Cook for 20 minutes to seal the meat.

Reduce the temperature to 190C/375F/Gas mark 5

Cook for 15 minutes per lb (30 mins per kg).

Baste occasionally.

Plus 15 mins for medium rare.

Plus 30 mins for well done.

Remove from oven and place in a warming oven for 30 mins to relax.

Make a gravy from the meat juices by stirring in flour to thicken, add a stock cube if desired and dilute using water from what ever vegetables you are cooking to accompany the meat.

Reheat the oven for the last 30 mins to cook the Yorkshire puddings and crisp the roast potatoes.

YORKSHIRE PUDDING

Place the flour in a bowl and add the eggs and a little milk.

Mix to a thick batter. With the bowl tilted, beat the batter until it is full of bubbles (5 mins). Leave it to rest for 30 minutes.

Add a little more milk and beat again for 5 minutes.

Add more milk until batter is thin but not as thin as pancake batter.

TINS: There are three different ways of cooking Yorkshire puds.

Yorkshire pudding tins, approx 4" in diameter. 1 tray makes 4 puddings. Jam tart trays makes lots of little puds. The roasting tin that the meat and gravy have just been removed from.

Put the tin in the oven with a little oil or fat, and heat until the oil is very hot.

Pour in the batter and cook in a hot oven for approx 10 to 15 minutes. If you use the roasting tin cut the pudding into portions. Serve with the roast meat and gravy.

ROAST POTATOES. Cooking time 1½ hours approx.

Peel and quarter the potatoes. Put them into cold water with a little salt and bring to the boil.

Simmer for 10 minutes or until they are just starting to go soft round the edges.

Drain and brush with vegetable oil, place around the joint of meat. Baste occasionally.

Turn over after 1 hour. This also works with parsnips (cut in half) swede (cubed) turnip (cubed) and pumpkin.

Buy the best and biggest joint of beef that you can afford.

YORKSHIRE PUDDING
4 tblsp of plain flour
2 medium eggs
milk
fat or oil
Makes 4 large or 8+ small puddings

Hardwick/Sutton

KLAUS LUDWIG

ROAST HAUNCH OF WILD BOAR

1998 FIA GT Champion, Mercedes

1 haunch (leg) of wild boar
1 tablespoon of coarse salt,
rosemary, juniper berries,
coriander, dry mustard,
lemon juice
vegetables

Remove the skin in one piece, trim off excess fat.

Grind herbs and spices together into a paste. Rub it into the meat, replace the skin and leave for at least a couple of hours or over-night.

Preheat the oven to 150C/300F/Gas Mark 2.

Place the haunch in a large roasting tin.

Roast for 30 mins per 1lb (450g).

Parboil root vegetables, potatoes, swede, parsnip, celeriac.

Place them round the joint for the last hour.

Add 20 mins to the cooking time and increase oven to 200C/400F/Gas Mark 6.

Allow the meat to rest for 20 mins, discard the skin and carve the meat into thin slices.

Make a gravy with the meat juices.

Serve with the roast vegetables.

FORMULA ONE MINCE AND TATTIES

1989 British Formula Ford 1600 Champion
McLaren Autosport BRDC Winner
1994-1999 Formula 1 Driver: Williams, McLaren
Grand Prix wins: 4

Formula 1 Driver: McLaren
This is the winning recipe on
Celebrity Ready Steady Cook – Chef, Paul Rankin
BBC1 Television Jan 21st 1998

Sporting Pictures (UK)

Place the swede in a bowl and add the white wine vinegar, caster sugar and a pinch of salt, leave to marinate for about 15 minutes. After marinating, drain and sprinkle with chilli powder.

Cook the potatoes in boiling salted water until tender. When cooked, mash or pass through a potato ricer. Add the milk and seasoning, mix and keep warm.

Heat 25g/1oz butter and 1 tblsp vegetable oil in a pan. Add the mince and half the onion and cook for about 10 minutes or until brown. Add the stock to the mince and onion, bring to the boil, simmer for 5-8 minutes until the mince is thoroughly cooked. Season.

Cut the parsnips into 4cm pieces then 'turn' (trim with sharp knife to round off edges and make barrel shape). Heat 25g/1oz butter and olive oil in a frying pan, add the parsnip and cook over a medium heat for about 10/15 minutes or until tender and golden brown.

Slice the remaining onion, sprinkle over $\frac{1}{4}$ tsp salt and toss in the flour, shake off excess. Fill a deep pan one third full with vegetable oil and heat. When hot, deep fry the onions until golden and crisp and remove.

Deep fry cabbage in batches until crisp, drain on kitchen paper.

Spoon the potatoes into a piping bag and pipe on to a serving plate in the shape of a chequered flag. Spoon the mince onto potatoes and serve with parsnips, pickled swede, deep fried onion and cabbage.

I onion, sliced
300ml /¹/₂pt beef stock
2 parsnips, peeled
1 tsp olive oil
25g / 1oz flour
Savoy cabbage quarter, finely shredded
100g / 3 ¹/₂oz thinly sliced swede
100ml/ 3 ¹/₂ fl oz white wine vinegar
4 tsp caster sugar
¹/₄ tsp chilli powder
2 potatoes, peeled, chopped into cubes
50ml /2 fl oz milk
55g/2oz butter
1 tblsp vegetable oil, extra for frying
9oz extra lean minced beef
salt and pepper

JUDY GANLEY

PIRI PIRI CHICKEN (FROM PORTUGAL)

Raced in USA as Judy Kondratieff.
Raced a Bugeye Sprite and Mini Cooper S in C Sedan Class, 3rd in class in 1968
1st in under 2 litre class, Sebring 12 Hours,1970 with Ring Free Oil All Girls Team
Doghouse Chairman, Vice-Chairman and Treasurer
Patron, The Doghouse Owners' Club
Lady Captain and Handicap Secretary of Ladies Section of Maidenhead Golf Club

1 tblsp Hot chilli sauce (or to taste)

1 tblsp rock salt

2 tsp Swartz piri piri mix per lb of chicken

2 tsp fresh squeezed lemon juice per lb of chicken

2 tblsp sunflower or vegetable oil per lb of chicken

crushed chilli pepper to taste (I use a lot)

2 medium (3lb) chickens (cut into about 16 pieces)

Mix together the first six ingredients in a bowl and stir well so that powders and salt liquefy.

Place the chicken pieces in ovenproof dishes and cover with the marinade.

Let stand in fridge for a couple of hours or overnight.

Place all in a pre-heated oven 375F/Gas mark 6.

Cook for about 40 minutes and remove from oven.

Drain off the marinade from the chicken into a bowl and keep warm.

Barbecue the chicken pieces over medium coals until golden brown.

Replace in ovenproof dish, pour over hot marinade and serve with plenty of napkins.

Serving ideas: tomato and red onion salad, hot Ciabatta bread, crisp oven fried American style crisps. Delicious!

MIKE AND ANNE KIMPTON

GINGER AND ORANGE MARINATED LAMB

Mike raced a Lola and Tiga Sports 2000 from 1977 to '80, a Capri and Mazda
Group 1 Saloons '80-'82, Tiga Thundersports '80-'82, Tiga World Sports Cars '82-'89
and a Sierra Cosworth RS 500 in Group N Saloons '88-'90.
Anne is a Ceramicist and Teacher and one of the Racey Recipe Collaborators.

1 large leg of lamb, 2 inches of fresh root ginger

MARINADE

16 fl oz fresh orange juice from a carton, 4 tblsp clear honey

4 tblsp soy sauce, 4 tblsp vinegar, 4 cloves of garlic - crushed

4 heaped teaspoons of dried rosemary, 2 tsp of ground ginger

orange wedges and fresh rosemary to garnish

This is a wonderful easy dinner party dish as well as a great Sunday lunch! The whole thing can be prepared well in advance (even left to marinate over a racing weekend!!) and thrown into the Aga when needed.

Make up the marinade by mixing all the ingredients together in a bowl and then pouring it into two plastic bags (inside each other) which will be big enough to hold the leg of lamb easily.

Peel the fresh ginger and slice into slivers, then make small slits in the skin of the lamb and push the ginger slivers into them.

Place the lamb into the marinade in the plastic bags.

Seal the bags by tying them tightly together, and then place in a roasting tin.

Give the lamb a few turns to make sure it is well soaked in the marinade, and then leave for as long as you like, but at least 24 hours.

When you are ready to cook the lamb, remove from bag and place it in the roasting tin and cook at 180C for 20 minutes, or in the top oven of an Aga. Then turn the oven down to 160C, or transfer to the baking oven if you have a 4 oven Aga.

Add the marinade to the lamb and baste thoroughly.

Cook for 15 minutes per pound (for medium/rare) or 20 minutes per pound if you like it well done.

The marinade will turn into a dark, rich gravy and all you need to do is skim off any fat and it is ready to serve.

Garnish the lamb with some thinly sliced oranges, and serve with a good Potato Dauphinoise which can be cooked in the oven at the same time as the lamb, and there you have it- a truly delicious meal!

A veteran of more than 200 BTCC races, John Cleland was champion in 1989 and 1995. Coming from the old school he turns a blind eye to all this new-fangled fitness stuff, preferring to eat and drink what he wants – and he still knows how to win! "As I always have a curry before races, it makes me rush back! This is a delicately flavoured curry and very popular in the mad Cleland household."

JOHN CLELAND

ROGHAN GOSHT

British Touring Car Championship Driver Vauxhall Vectra

Rose/Sutton

Combine the yoghurt, Asafoetida and cayenne in a large bowl and stir in the meat cubes.

Cover and set aside.

Put the ginger, garlic, spices and almonds in a blender with 4 tablespoons of water and blend to a smooth purée. Transfer to a small bowl.

Melt the ghee or clarified butter in a flameproof casserole.

Add the onion and fry, stirring occasionally, until it is golden brown.

Stir in the turmeric and spice purée and fry for 8 minutes, stirring constantly.

Add the lamb cubes and yoghurt mixture and fry until the cubes are evenly browned.

Cover the casserole, reduce to low heat and simmer for 45 minutes.

Preheat the oven to 140C/Gas mark 1/275F.

Uncover the casserole and stir in 50ml (2 fl oz) or ¼ cup of water.

Add another 50ml of water and stir until it has been absorbed. Pour in the remaining water.

Cover the casserole and reduce the heat to low. Simmer for a further 15 minutes.

Stir in the garam masala and coriander leaves.

Cover the casserole and put in the oven. Cook for 25 minutes.

Transfer to a warmed serving dish and serve at once.

Serves 4-6
Preparation and cooking time
1¾ hours

250ml (8fl oz) yoghurt
¼ tsp Asafoetida
1 tsp cayenne pepper
1 kg (2 lbs) lean lamb, cubed
4cm (2 inch) piece of fresh root ginger, peeled and chopped
4 garlic cloves
1 tsp white poppy seeds
1 tsp cumin seeds
1 tblsp coriander seeds
4 cloves
2 tblsp cardomon seeds
8 peppercorns
2 tblsp unblanched almonds
50g (2oz) ghee or clarified butter
1 medium onion, chopped
1 tsp turmeric
250ml water
1 tsp garam masala
1 tblsp chopped coriander leaves

Lynton Money

CHILLI CON CARNE

Ex-wife of LES LESTON
"Les seems to have driven just about everything in the '50s and early '60s including: Cooper, Connaught, BRM, Aston Martin and Lotus." Doreen told Racey Recipes.

Serves 4
Peheat oven to 300F Gas mark 2
1lb minced beef
2 medium onions
1 fat garlic clove
2 heaped tblsp tomato purée
1 rounded tblsp flour
1 medium tin red kidney beans
1 green pepper, de-seeded and chopped
1 level tsp dried chilli powder (or to taste)
salt, freshly ground black pepper
red wine to taste, add water to make up to 1 pint
Olive oil

Method:

In a flame proof casserole dish, gently cook diced onions and crushed garlic in a tablespoon of olive oil for about 6 mins.

Turn up the heat, add beef and brown it stirring all the time.

Add the flour and stir in to soak up the juices.

Mix the tomato purée with the red wine and water.

Add gradually to the meat and onions.

Add the chilli, drain the kidney beans and rinse in cold water and add.

Bring to simmering point, cover and cook for about 1½ hours.

Add the peppers and cook for a further 30 mins.

Serve with white rice, hot french garlic bread, various chutneys and soured cream.

A great party dish which can be eaten with a fork.

Les has always been someone who acts on impulse, so when he decided we should get a cottage in the country, that is what we did. When there wasn't any racing, we would pile in the car with children, Nicholas and Kimberley, children's friends, food and heaven only knows what else and go off for a nice 'quiet' weekend. Quiet, was hardly how I would describe these outings, unexpected guests would pop in having been invited by Les, who had forgotten to tell me. Our impromptu parties were famous in motor racing circles. I rarely had time to sit and enjoy my lovely country garden.

I love to cook and even did a Cordon Bleu course to try out new and different dishes. We lived in St John's Wood which was well supplied with delicatessens and I also shopped in Soho for interesting ingredients. I think it was here I discovered Chilli con Carné. I found it was an ideal basic dish when catering for a large party. It wasn't as common then as it is now, most probably because chilli was not so readily available. It was considered rather trendy!

One weekend the cottage was full of friends as there was a race meeting at Brands Hatch, which was not far away. I was rushing around making up beds, serving drinks and trying to get the food ready as the party had grown during the day. Graham and Bette Hill had come over from their nearby cottage with their three children, Damon, Brigitte and Samantha. Jim Clark and Peter Jopp were staying as they were going on to Brands, Sir Gawaine Baillie had popped in as had Sir John and Gunilla Whitmore. They were racing Ford Falcons the next day.

The chilli was in a large pan on the top of the stove and Les would keep coming into my kitchen and telling me how I was doing it all wrong and how it needed more seasoning. While I was out of the room he added more chilli, when I returned I decided that I had better humour him and also added more. The result was explosive. Half the guests were squeezed into the kitchen drinking straight from the tap while the rest were scattered around the upstairs bathrooms. The following morning they kept on leaving and then reappearing to dash to the loo. I shall never look at chilli con carné without remembering that party.

The moral is, check the seasoning before serving.

EASTERN STIR FRY PORK (OR BEEF)

Wife of the late Graham Hill OBE., (Triple Crown Winner - Formula 1 World Champion 1962, 1968; Indianapolis 500 and Le Mans 24 Hours Winner) Mother of Damon Hill OBE., (Formula 1 World Champion 1996) President, The Doghouse Owners' Club

Lynton Money

Put meat in a shallow dish.

Mix sherry, soy sauce, and pour over meat. Put in refrigerator for at least 1 hour.

Slice carrots and leeks.

Heat oil in frying pan, remove meat from marinade and fry until browned.

When the meat is cooked, remove from pan and keep warm.

Add leek, carrot and ginger and stir fry for 4 mins.

Add pepper, sugar, water, marinade and the meat. Simmer for 10 mins.

Add peas. Mix vinegar and cornflour and add, to thicken the sauce, keep stirring.

Serve with rice or noodles.

Serves 4
1lb (450g) pork fillet (or beef)
1 sliced green pepper, de-seeded
1 carrot
6oz (180g) frozen peas
1 leek
a small piece of grated fresh ginger
3 tblsp soy sauce (or to taste)
2 tblsp dry sherry
2 tblsp vegetable oil
1 tsp light brown sugar
3 tblsp white wine vinegar
7 fl oz water
2 tsp cornflour
salt and pepper

ESCALOPES OF VEAL BROWNIE

Caterer for ASTON MARTIN

2 x 5oz escalopes of veal
1oz plain flour
2oz unsalted butter
2oz thinly sliced mushrooms
2 to 3 fluid oz dry white wine
5 fluid oz double cream
4 fluid oz veal or chicken stock
wedge of lemon
1 clove of crushed garlic
1 tsp bay leaf powder
1 tsp chopped parsley

For anyone with strong feelings about veal, pork loin may be subsituted, boned and beaten thin and cooked in exactly the same way.

Select a low heat and melt the butter in a shallow pan.

Add the mushrooms and squeeze over the lemon juice.

Sieve the flour onto a dinner plate, grind in the black pepper and salt together with the bay leaf powder.

Between cling film, beat the escalopes until thin and trim off any untidy edges or fat.

Dredge both sides in the flour mixture and lightly smear with garlic.

Increase the heat and cook the escalopes for 3 minutes either side.

Add the wine and stock at intervals, reduce heat.

Allow to reduce slightly, pour in the cream and when bubbling smother the escalopes in the sauce.

Sprinkle with chopped parsley.

I catered for the 24 Hours race at Le Mans on four different occasions. Of course the cake was iced when Aston Martin were first and second in 1959.

Page 44 of Stirling Moss's book 'Le Mans '59' more or less sums up the operation and the illustration of the race cars transporter which incorporated my rather primitive kitchen.

Nevertheless, it produced over 450 menus and hundreds of beverages during the practice and race periods, and seemed to attract personalities from competitors teams. Bless them.

Le Diner for the evening of June 20th 1959

Chirontais Melon

Turtle Soup with Sherry

Escalope of Veal 'Brownie'

Petits pois Francaise, New potatoes

Cheeses

Strawberries and Cream

Coffee with Bendict Mints

1984 European Formula 3 Champion, Coloni
1986 Formula 3000 Champion, Genoa Racing
1985-1993 Formula 1 Driver: Tyrrell, AGS, March,
Leyton House, Ferrari and Jordan.

MEATBALLS WITH TOMATO SAUCE
POLPETTE CON SUGO DI POMMADORO

Formula 1 reporter/presenter, Italian television
Racey Recipes caught up with him at Silverstone, pinned him to the pit-wall
until he gave up and gave us what we wanted, this recipe ....

Sporting Pictures (UK)

Mix the meat, onions, eggs and breadcrumbs, garlic, cayenne, salt and pepper together in a bowl. If the mixture is too soft, add more breadcrumbs.

Put a little flour on your hands and divide the meat mixture into 8.
Roll the meat mixture into 8 slightly flattened balls.

Heat the oil in a frying pan and fry the meatballs for 6 to 8 minutes, turning once.
Remove from the pan and keep warm.

Pour off some of the oil in which you have fried the meatballs.
Add a little virgin olive oil and fry the chopped onion.
When onion is golden, add garlic and the skinned and cored tomatoes.
Cook over a medium heat until the tomatoes are broken down.

Season with the basil leaves, salt and pepper.

Serve the meatballs with the tomato sauce.

2 lbs (1kg) minced beef
6oz (180g) fresh breadcrumbs
2 eggs, beaten
2 onions, finely chopped
1 or 2 cloves of garlic as desired
1 tsp cayenne pepper
salt and fresh ground black pepper
oil for frying
flour for dusting

Tomato sauce
8 or 10 large plum tomatoes
(or you can use canned)
1 onion, finely chopped
1 clove of garlic
a good bunch of fresh basil
extra virgin olive oil
salt and fresh ground black pepper

SALLY BARKING MAD (Pork with Apricots)

Steve raced: Formula 2 Cooper Climax, Lotus Formula Junior, Ausper Formula Junior, Alexis Formula Junior, Willment Climax Sports Car

Serves 4
1lb (480g) rib of pork (diced)
1 large green pepper
1 large onion
2 tablespoon Worcestershire sauce
2 tablespoon white wine vinegar
1/2 pint (300ml) chicken stock
(1 chicken stock cube 1/2 pint water)
2 teaspoon tomato purée
1 tin of apricot halves
1 or 2 tablespoons of cornflour to thicken
4oz dark brown sugar

Cut up the onion and green pepper and place in a large saucepan, cook until soft in a little oil and butter.

Add the diced pork and cook over a gentle heat.

Add the apricot juice (not the apricots).

Add the rest of ingredients, cover and cook over a low heat for 45 minutes stirring occasionally, add seasoning to taste.

Add the cornflour to thicken and then add the apricot halves.

Cook for a further 15 minutes.

Serve this delicious sweet and sour dish with creamed mashed potatoes or rice and french beans.

Happy Cooking!

WILL HOY

A Touring Car Champion in Japan and Le Mans regular.
BTCC driver with BMW, Williams, Ford
BTC Champion Williams 1991
GT Championship, Dodge Viper, 1999

EVERYTHING YOU HAVE HEARD ABOUT THE TOURING CAR MEN APPEARS TO BE TRUE!

This is one of the more printable stories. We are away so much in the company of competitive individuals and pranksters.

One of the best, particularly for the participants on the night which included drivers, John Cleland, Paul Radisich, Jeff Allam and Tim Harvey, was a scam we pulled on Alan Gow, head of BTCC organiser TOCA.

We were at a smart hotel restaurant at a table of 10 and on one of Alan Gow's smoking exeats, I borrowed a credit card from his wallet and we hatched a plan. We agreed that John Cleland would pretend that Vauxhall had given him free credit on his Vauxhall/GM credit card (who were sponsoring his car) and he thereby offered to pay for everybody's meal - a total of £380.

Alan fell for this kind offer and at the end of the meal, John presented Alan's card to the restaurant which was duly accepted. As if to compound the sting even further, Alan actually offered to give some cash to John but he gallantly declined to accept, believing a double hit would have made our lives even harder at future BTCC rounds!

Apart from the problem of having to suppress our laughter, we had the added problem of getting Alan's card back into his wallet since he had put his jacket back on. We all retired to the snooker room where I challenged Alan to a game and he promptly removed his jacket and someone slipped the credit card back into his wallet whilst he was taking a shot. We all retired to bed giggling like schoolboys.

The shit hit the fan big time about four weeks later when Alan rang to give us major verbal abuse! Just to add to the 'hit' Alan unfortunately paid this particular credit card by direct debit so he had no chance to query it. Needless to say all restaurant outings are now fairly nervous affairs with nobody careless enough to leave a wallet unattended! As you can imagine, we suddenly found ourselves making inordinately numerous visits to the weighbridge during qualifying for the rest of the season so Alan sort of got his own back.

FAVOURITE RESTAURANTS

MAX WILSON

Max's favourite restaurant is FOGO DE CHAO, in SAO PAULO, BRAZIL.

Avenue Santo Amaro, 6824 - Santo Amaro, tel 55-11-247.8786.

Avenue Moreira Guimaraes, 9644 - Indianopolis, tel 55-11-530.2795.

ALSO AT PORTO ALEGRE, BRAZIL

Avenue Cavalhada, 5200 - Ipanema, tel 55-51-248.3940.

AND AT DALLAS, TEXAS, U.S.A.

4300 Beltline Road, Addison, Texas 75244 . Tel (972) 503.7300.

Churrasco is a traditional way of cooking meat first used by the gauchos who pierced big pieces of meat and cooked them round a fire burning in a pit. At the FOGO DE CHAO they prepare meat in the same way and serve it with salad.

DON and JOANNE NAMAN

Executive Director of the International Motor Sports Hall of Fame, Talladega.

NASCAR Café, Nashville, Tennessee.

It is a great place to eat and enjoy numerous racing exhibits, photos, games and memorabilia.

NICK MASON

Nick's favourite restaurant in London is the Mirabelle.

KEN AND NORAH TYRRELL

NICHOLAS, 2072 Drummond, Montreal, Canada

LES LESTON

Robbie's in Estepona, Spain.

Spicy Pasta Penne
Ralf Schumacher

Caesar Salad
Alan Minshaw

Spaghetti Carbonara
Mario Haberfeld and Pedro Lamy

Mozzarella
Phil Hill

Italian Minestrone
Alain Prost

pasta

Sporting Pictures (UK)

SONIA IRVINE

LINGUINI WITH FRESH STEAMED VEGETABLES AND TOMATO SAUCE

Sister of Eddie and his Personal Physiotherapist

'The dish I enjoy cooking the most is a Pomadoro sauce which I have learnt to make in Italy. It is a basic tomato sauce which I use for a lot of dishes but especially pasta.'

fresh ripe tomatoes
salt and pepper
good olive oil
sugar to taste
lots of fresh basil, chopped

Simmer tomatoes in the oil with seasoning and sugar until soft, add the basil.

STEAMED VEGETABLES

Place small fresh firm vegetables in a steamer or a metal colander fitted into a lidded saucepan.

Cook over boiling water until just cooked but still crunchy.

Onions, green beans and broccoli all work well.

LINGUINI

Cook the pasta in boiling salted water with a little olive oil to stop it sticking.

RED FLAG WARNING! PASTA MUST BE 'AL DENTE' do not overcook.

Toss some mushrooms in a little oil and cook briefly. Add the vegetables to the linguini and mix together.

JACKIE AND HELEN STEWART

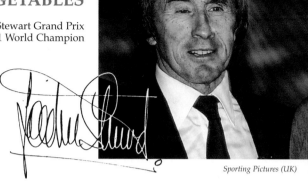

Sporting Pictures (UK)

HELEN'S FETTUCCINI AND VEGETABLES

Jackie Stewart OBE Executive Chairman, Stewart Grand Prix
Triple Formula 1 World Champion

The World Champion driver in 1969, 1971 and 1973 and winner of 27 of his 99 Grand Prix. During his racing career, which developed with spectacular speed once Ken Tyrrell had talent-spotted him for one of his Formula 3 Cooper-BMCs, Stewart became an eloquent ambassador for the sport and a leading figure in the campaign to improve safety standards. Since retiring from the cockpit at the end of 1973 he retained close links with the sport in the role of international business consultant and TV commentator and in 1997 returned as Executive Chairman of Stewart Grand Prix, working with his son Paul and Ford to field two increasingly competitive cars for Rubens Barrichello and Johnny Herbert.

JOHN BLUNSDEN Journalist

Put a pan of salted water on to boil for the fettuccini.

Put the crushed garlic, sliced anchovies and thinly sliced chillies in the oil in a large pan over a low heat for approx 2 mins.

If the anchovy flavour is too strong, soak them in milk. Chilli seeds are the hottest bit, use them to your taste.

Slice the broccoli thinly and discard any tough stalks.
Add to the pan and stir fry for 2 or 3 mins.

Cut the asparagus into 3cm lengths.
Add the asparagus and rocket to the pan and cook until the asparagus is cooked, about another 2 mins.

Cook the fettuccini until 'al dente' do not over cook.
Pile the pasta into a large dish, season with freshly ground black pepper. Cover with sauce.

Serve with a green salad.

500 gm fettuccini
broccoli florets
small hot chillies
fresh asparagus
rocket
olive oil
2 cloves garlic
2 anchovy fillets
ground black pepper

74

Sutton

GIANCARLO FISICHELLA

BUCATINI ALL'AMATRICIANA (AMATRICE WAY)

Formula 1 Driver: Benetton

1994 Italian Formula 3 Champion
1996 Won Bologna F1 Supersprint, Benetton
1996-1999 Formula 1 Driver: Minardi, Jordan, Benetton

"As I say very often, I do not eat very much but I like very much to eat.

I like almost everything, meat, seafood etc., but a good portion of pasta is the thing I like most."

"Now before I write down this easy recipe, here is a little history. Amatrice is a little village, in the centre of Italy and in the last centuries used to be a crossroads for shepherds during their migration with their sheep. From there, with the simple ingredients a shepherd could have, this recipe comes. For me, it is one of the most tasteful ways to prepare pasta."

For 4 people you need:
1 big onion
100g of guanciale (this is a kind of un-smoked bacon made with the cheek of pork)
400g of peeled tomatoes
400g of bucatini
(larger spaghetti with a hole inside)
some Pecorino cheese (hard cheese with at least 50% sheep milk)
olive oil, salt and pepper

In a tall pot you put water with a fistful of salt to boil for the pasta.

In a frying pan you put a little olive oil and the chopped onion and the guanciale, if you can not get this then bacon will be OK. Cut into narrow slices and fry. When both the onion and the guanciale pieces look golden coloured, put in the peeled tomatoes, breaking them down with a wooden spoon while they cook.

After 5 to 10 minutes when all the water from the tomatoes has evaporated it will look like a uniform sauce and will be ready.

In the meantime, when the water boils put in the bucatini, when it is cooked (read the instructions, some pasta cooks in 8 minutes, some take longer). Strain it very well.

Put the pasta in a bowl, put on the sauce and mix together.

Grate on the pecorino cheese. Just a little grated black pepper and ... enjoy it.

All the best,

Giancarlo Fisichella

1983-1995 Multiple Kart Champion
1995-1996 German Formula 3 Championship
1996 German Formula 3 Champion (Benetton Jnr. Team)
1997-1999 Formula 1 Driver: Minardi, Prost

*Jarno adores home made pizza like those made by his
aunt in Italy. We looked, we searched high and low,
we really did and still we could not find his aunt, so
this is not her actual recipe.*

JARNO TRULLI

PIZZA BLANCA

Formula 1: Driver Prost

Prost GP

Grease a large pizza tin.

Sieve the flour into a large bowl and stir in the herbs.

Season with salt and pepper.

Stir in the yeast.

Add the oil and blend in half the water adding more if necessary
to form a stiff dough.

Knead well on a lightly floured board until smooth and elastic.

Press into a 10 inch/25cm circle and put onto the tin.

Cover with a cloth or cling film and leave in a warm place for
the dough to rise approx 30 minutes.

TOPPING

Heat the oil in a frying pan. Add the onion, thinly sliced. Cook
until soft.

Arrange on the prepared pizza base.

Dice the prosciutto and arrange on top of the onion.

Top with the grated Mozzarella.

Bake for 10/15 minutes in a pre-heated oven at 230C/450F/Gas
mark 8.

BASIC PIZZA DOUGH
Makes one 10 inch pizza

8oz (225g) strong white flour
1 tsp chopped fresh basil
1 tsp chopped fresh parsley
1 tsp dried yeast
1 tsp olive oil
$\frac{1}{4}$ pint (150ml) warm water

TOPPING
1 onion
2oz Prosciutto, Parma ham or Salami
2oz Mozzarella cheese, grated
1 tsp olive oil

ALESSANDRO ZANARDI

PASTA WITH BROCCOLI

Formula 1 Driver: Williams

Sporting Pictures (UK)

*1991 – 1994 Formula 1 Driver: Jordan,
Minardi, Lotus
1995 Sports car driver: Porsche Supercup
1996 'Rookie of the Year' ChampCar,
Chip Ganassi Racing
1997 ChampCar World Champion,
Chip Ganassi Racing
1998 ChampCar World Champion,
Chip Ganassi Racing*

*After a hectic day's testing his Williams at Kyalami
in preparation for the 1999 Australian Grand Prix,
Alex sent us his recipe, adding: 'This is really good if
you have to do a work-out in the afternoon or if you
have to drive and you want some powerful fuel to
put in your stomach that is not so heavy and tough
to burn.....'*

**broccoli
garlic
extra virgin olive oil
anchovy
one small chilli**

You boil the flower of the broccoli until it gets a bit soft, then, in a pan you put just a touch of extra virgin olive oil with two cloves of garlic. Not chopped, just the cloves, which you must remove later.

Add one anchovy and a little chilli.

Heat the oil a little bit and stir the anchovy until it melts in the oil. Then, you let it cook down and you take the broccoli you've boiled and put it in the pan.

Boil the pasta in the water you boiled the broccoli in beforehand.

Take the pasta off, drain it and mix everything together on the heat for another five minutes and it's ready to eat – and it's good!!

RALF SCHUMACHER

SPICY PENNE PASTA

Formula One Driver Williams

Sporting Pictures (UK)

1991 German Junior Kart Champion
1995 Winner of the prestigious Macau Formula 3 race
1996 1st - All Nippon Japanese Formula 3000
Championship (2 Wins)
Career best: 2nd Belgian Grand Prix, 3rd Italian
Grand Prix with Jordan (1998)

Heat the oil in a pan and fry the chopped onion and crushed garlic until soft.

Add the tomatoes, tomato purée and chilli and season with salt and pepper to taste.

Leave to simmer while you cook the pasta in a large pan of boiling salted water until it is 'al dente' (tender but still firm).

Drain the pasta and toss in the hot sauce, garnish with the basil leaves.

Ralf likes to drink apple juice mixed with sparkling water with his meal.

1 medium onion, chopped
1 garlic clove, crushed
1 red chilli, de-seeded and finely chopped
3 large tomatoes, skinned and chopped (or 1 tin of chopped tomatoes)
1 tsp of tomato paste
2 tsp of olive oil
several chopped fresh basil leaves
salt and fresh ground black pepper
approx 3 oz (90gm) penne pasta per person

Sporting Pictures (UK)

JEAN TODT

PASTA ALL'OLIO DI OLIVA E PARMIGGIANO PASTA WITH OLIVE OIL AND PARMESAN CHEESE

Team Sporting Director, Ferrari

Eddie Irvine wins 1999 Australian G.P.

Sporting Pictures (UK)

Sift the flour into a large bowl or onto a work surface.

Make a well and add the eggs and oil.

Fold the flour into the eggs with your fingers and when combined into a ball, knead for 10 minutes. The pasta should be smooth and elastic.

Process the pasta according to the instructions of your pasta machine.

Place over a rolling pin and allow to dry for 30 minutes.

Cook in boiling salted water for approx. 5 minutes or until 'al dente'.

Drain and toss in the best olive oil, grated fresh parmesan cheese and fresh ground black pepper.

PASTA
1 lb (500g) strong OO flour
4 eggs
1 tsp oil
salt

Prior to his present position, Jean headed the entire motor sport programme for Automobiles Peugeot (for twelve years); accomplished major successes in the World Rally Championship (2 Drivers' and 2 Constructors' titles); 4 Paris-Dakar victories; the World Sports Car Championship and Le Mans 24 Hours. Jean won a World Rally Championship title himself, as a co-driver.

Minardi

TAGLIATELLE DI NONNA ELSA
GRANDMA ELSA'S TAGLIATELLE
by Gianni a "Pinotto" Cenni

Formula 1 Constructor, Minardi

1985 Minardi was founded
Best results:
1991 7th in Constructors Championship, 4th San Marino & Portugese Grands Prix
1993 4th South African Grand Prix

The Minardi Team is well respected in the Formula 1 paddock for its passion, charm, seriously good coffee, but above all, for its total professionalism.

Grandma Elsa, a.k.a. Elsa Renzi Bucci, is Gian Carlo Minardi's mother-in-law who, contrary to the norm, has a special relationship with her son-in-law. When Gian Carlo is not at races this recipe is his standard Sunday fare. With it he recommends Sangiovese, the local red wine.

Finely chop the celery, carrot and onion and lightly fry in olive oil.

Add the minced beef and sausage and stir thoroughly for one minute.

Pour over a dash of white wine. Simmer off the excess liquid then stir in the milk and simmer gently for 45 minutes. Stir occasionally and finally stir in the tomatoes.
Season with salt and pepper.

Meanwhile, cook the tagliatelle in boiling water with a pinch of salt.

Strain when cooked and add to the pan with the finished sauce.

Stir well and serve.

Serves 4
600g fresh tagliatelle
(if you don't have Grandma Elsa's then Barilla will do)
150g prime minced beef
100g fresh sausage
400g tomatoes, fresh or tinned
extra virgin olive oil
half a cup of full fat fresh milk
white wine
celery, carrot and onion

Gianni a "Pinotto" Cenni

MAURICIO AND STELLA GUGELMIN

■■■■■■■■■■■■■■■■■■■■■■■■■

TORTELLINI ALLA PANNA

Mauricio Gugelmin Champ Car Driver: PacWest

1980 Brazilian Kart Champion
1981 Brazilian Formula Fiat Champion
1984 European Formula Ford 2000 Champion
1985 British Formula 3 Champion
1988-1991 Formula 1 Driver: March, Jordan
1993 Champ Car Driver: Dick Simon Racing
1994-1999 Champ Car Driver: PacWest

This is Mauricio's favourite dish which we learnt when we had Italian lessons with a private tutor when we were living in England some years ago. She was Italian and gave us this favourite recipe.

Mix cream, Parmesan cheese, pepper and butter in a bowl until thick. Put a plate to heat in the oven. Cook the pasta for the time stated on the packet. When the pasta is cooked, mix in the cream mixture and sprinkle some fresh parsley on the top.

Serves 2
Cooking time: 10 minutes

Ingredients:

I packet of tortellini
¹/₂ pint of whipping cream
1 ounce of Parmesan cheese
¹/₂ ounce of unsalted butter
fresh parsley
black pepper

DON GRANT
LEFT OVERS

My mother, Eba, had a curious, squirrel-like habit of keeping left-overs in ramekins, cups without handles and orphaned saucers - four baked beans, an egg yolk, two small boiled potatoes, that sort of thing - they would sit in the fridge for days. In the case of the egg yolk, it would eventually solidify to such an extent that the egg and the cup would inevitably be consigned to the bin. I agree with the sentiments of Herb Shriner, who once stated that his wife did wonderful things with left-overs.........she threw them out.

JOHNNY SAVOURS HIS BACON

Johnny Herbert regularly sits down in the Formula 1 paddock, to eat a disgustingly healthy breakfast of muesli and yoghurt, once that is out of the way and his trainer Joseph is not looking, he sneaks down to the Ford Motorhome for one of Stuart and Di Spires's bacon or sausage sandwiches. I think it is probably the main reason he has signed for Stewart Ford for 1999.

JOE SAWARD, Journalist

MORETTI SPAGHETTI

5 times Winner Le Mans 24 Hours
1968 – 1974 Formula 1 Driver: Ferrari, McLaren, Brabham, Surtees, Techno
GT Driver: Porsche, Ferrari, Nissan, Chevrolet, McLaren
1985 World Endurance Champion

Sporting Pictures (UK)

This is obviously a pasta dish that can be changed around in various ways. The reason it is called "Moretti's' is that since the early eighties, when Gian Piero Moretti (a very dear racing driver friend) turned up at the circuits, the first thing out of his transporter was this giant cooker so that he could make his pasta for himself, his crew and friends! Yes, the cooker came out even before the car. We always looked forward to joining him on practice days and race days for lunch, it was just so good!

Eventually he decided to tell my wife, Misti, how to make the sauce, a very simple but wonderful sauce that made all the difference in this pasta dish. So, whenever I get asked what I would prefer for dinner – why "Moretti' Spaghetti' of course.

Derek likes his with a simple green salad. There are many other variations with this sauce but I'll leave you with just one.

When the sauce is simmering, nearer the end, add a travel size bottle (similar to what you aare given onboard an aeroplane) of Scotch. Once you remove the sauce from the heat, add cream, enough to just change the colour. This version is much richer in taste, but lovely!

Use enough oil to cover the bottom of a large saucepan and a bit more.

Sauté the onion for a few minutes then add the garlic and the chilli pepper, (the amount should be adjusted to your taste) it should be slightly spicy but not too hot.

Add the stock cube, either dissolved in a small amount of water or crushed straight in to the pan. Do not let the garlic cook too long, it will turn dark brown.

Add the tomatoes, the amount depends on how much you wish to make. I usually make extra and freeze it. It is wonderful thawed and reheated and saves time!

Bring to the boil, stirring frequently and then turn down the heat and let simmer for about an hour.

Cook your pasta according to directions – it should be 'al dente'. Strain the pasta leaving a small amount of water in the pasta (in other words, do not leave the pasta completely dry).

Add the butter, stirring to well coat the pasta then do the same with the Parmesan cheese.

Now, using a ladle, add enough sauce to fully coat your pasta and a bit more.

If you can leave it a few minutes it will make it all the better. Then serve!

Spaghetti or Penne (the amount depends on how many you are serving)
2 large tins of crushed tomatoes (if you can't get crushed, use tinned chopped tomatoes, purée them slightly and use with creamed tomatoes)
1 medium onion, finely chopped
1 large clove of garlic, crushed
approx. 1 tsp dried crushed chilli peppers
1 beef bouillon or stock cube
olive oil, Parmesan cheese, grated
1 tblsp butter or margarine

GISELLE SOHM

TOMATO AND BASIL SAUCE
FOR PASTA

Secretary of the Grand Prix Drivers Association (GPDA)

"I am sporty and like to keep fit. I go to the Loewes Hotel gym every day, where many of the drivers train. This pasta sauce is delicious and light, perfect for a hot summer night in Monte Carlo."

Giselle makes her sauce in a pestle and mortar or hand grinder. We think you could use an electric blender but the texture would not be so good.

Put gros sel (coarse sea salt) in mortar and grind with pestle.

Cut 2 or 3 cloves of garlic into small pieces with a hachoir.

Pull the leaves off a generous bunch of fresh basil, cut them up with scissors, grind in the pestle and mortar for approximately 1 minuute (consistency slightly coarser than a paste).

Peel and roughly chop raw tomatoes and add to the mixture. Grind a little and mix.

Add some good olive oil.

Add a lot of freshly grated Parmesan cheese.

The mixture should not be too runny or too thick.

Mix well, place in the fridge for 10 minutes.

Serve on fresh home made pasta.

PASTA EATERS

Pasta seems to be the staple diet for our current Formula 1 heroes, but Racey Recipes only allowed a few entries in this section to avoid being utterly pastadout!

RUBENS BARRICHELLO

Formula 1 Driver: Stewart
Won five national Karting titles
Won GM EuroSeries
Won British Formula 3 Championship
1993-1999 Formula 1 Driver: Jordan, Stewart

Rubens told us that he loves pasta like his Grandmother makes, however he didn't tell us what that was or where we could find his grandmother...........

BERND SCHNEIDER

Sports-Prototypes Driver: AMG Mercedes
1987 German Formula 3 Champion
1988-1989 Formula 1 Driver: Zakspeed
1990 Won Porsche Cup
1995 German Touring Car Champion
Winner of the International Touring Car Series with AMG Mercedes
1997 FIA GT Champion, AMG Mercedes

Bernd is a very fit and healthy guy, he told us that he likes pasta with tomato sauce and he drinks apple juice mixed with mineral water.

JUAN PABLO MONTOYA

CART Champ Car Driver Ganassi Racing
1998 FIA International F3000 Champion, Super Nova
Juan Pablo is taking the Champ Car scene by storm, having won three consecutive races in his 'rookie' year (1999).

Another health conscious driver who likes pasta and tomato.

SPAGHETTI CARBONARA

Formula 1 Test Driver (Honda), Formula 1 Driver, BAR

Sutton

1990 European Formula Ford Champion
1990 Runner-up (to Hakkinen) British Formula 3
Championship
1994-1999 Formula 1 Driver: Tyrrell, Arrows,
Honda- test driver
British American Racing (temporary driver)

Mika regularly cooks this in his own kitchen at his apartment in Chelsea.

Break two eggs in a heat resistant bowl.

Add some salt, plenty of pepper and some Parmesan cheese, six cloves of garlic and a piece of cut tarragon.

Fry fresh sliced champignons in a frying pan while cooking the spaghetti in water with some extra virgin olive oil added.

When the pasta is 'al dente' pour it over the mixture of eggs, add the mushrooms and break one more egg on top of the mixture and finally mix all well together.

There you have it, a pasta dish low in calories!

Sutton

NOEL EDMONDS

HAM AND BASIL PASTA

Television Celebrity and GT enthusiast

Despite his success on the small screen, Noel Edmonds has never lost his appetite for fast cars and motor sport. He raced a Cortina back in the Seventies and got involved in a GT team at the 1997 Le Mans 24-Hours. He now owns a splendid collection of classic cars.

Serves 4 or 5
2oz (60g) butter
6oz (180g) cooked lean ham
1 clove of garlic
1/2 pint double cream
20 fresh basil leaves
12oz (360g) pasta shapes
3 oz (90g) Parmesan cheese
salt and cayenne pepper

Melt half the butter and soften garlic clove.

Add chopped ham and simmer for 5 minutes.

Add cream and simmer for about 5 to 7 minutes until cream thickens.

Add seasoning and half the basil leaves (torn into smaller pieces).

Meanwhile, cook pasta in boiling salted water, drain and tip into a dish buttered with the remaining butter.

Add sauce and toss with 2oz of the grated Parmesan and the rest of the torn basil leaves.

Serve immediately with rest of the grated Parmesan handed around separately.

1984 British Formula Ford 1600 Junior Champion (25 victories)
    Grovewood Award Winner
1986 Formula Ford 2000 Champion
1991-1995 Formula 1 Driver: Brabham, Ligier, Tyrrell, McLaren
1992 Won Le Mans 24 Hours, Peugeot
Overall Valvoline Award Winner (Rookie-Season World Indy Car Series),
BRDC North American Award
1996-1998 Champ Car Driver: PacWest

MARK AND DEBORAH BLUNDELL

SPINACH FETTUCINE WITH SHRIMP ALFREDO

Mark Blundell Champ Car Driver PacWest

Dan R. Boyd

In addition to his racing career, Mark reports for Eurosport, BBC and Channel 5. He is also an ambassador for the Prince's Trust. Mark is a self-confessed chocaholic, loves Crunchy Bars and Cadbury's Dairy Milk chocolate. Sunday barbeques are a summertime essential.

Dan R. Boyd

A quick, light and healthy dish which combines my two favourite foods -seafood and pasta.

Method: Alfredo Sauce

Combine flour and garlic in a saucepan. Season with salt and pepper to taste.

Slowly stir in stock until smooth. Cook over medium high heat for 4 – 5 minutes, stirring constantly or until mixture boils and thickens.

Remove from heat and stir in yoghurt.

Toss with pasta and 4 tblsp cheese.

Sprinkle with parsley and remaining cheese.

Cook pasta in a pan of boiling water for 3 – 5 minutes until just al dente.

Drain well.

Combine shrimp and basil with basic sauce and serve over hot pasta.

Sprinkle with Parmesan.

SPINACH FETTUCINE WITH SHRIMP ALFREDO

6oz (170g) fresh spinach fettuccine
7$\frac{1}{2}$ oz (210g) Light Alfredo Sauce
4oz (110g) cooked shrimp
$\frac{1}{4}$ tsp dried basil (or a few fresh basil leaves if preferred)
1 tblsp grated or shaved Parmesan cheese

LIGHT ALFREDO SAUCE

4 tblsp flour
2 cloves chopped garlic
$\frac{3}{4}$ pint (390 ml) chicken stock
$\frac{1}{4}$ tsp pepper
5 tblsp plain yoghurt
6 tblsp grated Parmesan cheese
fresh chopped parsley

CONCHIGLIA CON BROCCOLI
Purple Sprouting Broccoli Sauce for Pasta

A Touring Car Champion in Japan and Le Mans regular
BTCC driver with BMW, Williams, Ford
BTC Champion Williams
GT Championship, Dodge Viper, 1999

**2 lbs broccoli heads and leaves
sea salt and black pepper
2 tblsp olive oil
3 large cloves garlic, sliced
2 small dried chillies, crushed
2oz (60g) butter
5 fl oz double cream
1 ½ oz anchovy fillets
2oz Parmesan cheese
3oz conchiglie or
any large shell pasta per person**

Cut the broccoli vertically into small pieces and blanch in boiling water for a minute.

Heat the olive oil and fry the garlic gently.

Add chilli, anchovies and butter and mash with a wooden spoon until garlic and anchovies soften and disintegrate.

Add the cream and broccoli and simmer for approximately 6 minutes.

Puree half the sauce and return to the pan and stir back in and season.

Stir the sauce into cooked pasta, conchiglie or any large pasta shells and serve with plenty of fresh grated Parmesan. You can also add more cream if desired.

PIZZA PASTA IN THE PITS

I have many stories about Eddie Jordan in his youth, but I know he will deny most of them. I knew him in Formula 3 days when he was still climbing down drainpipes to avoid having to pay the hotel bills. Usually, this was in the company of his driver at the time, Tommy Byrne (it was 1983). I used to live in the Eddie Jordan Racing truck and they would stay in fleapit hotels. I remember heading off with Tommy one night into Imola, to find some spaghetti and pizza for Eddie and the mechanics. We got very lost, which was normal with Tommy - but, we did eventually find the restaurant he was looking for and ordered the takeaway food. We then tried to deliver it back and I spent an uncomfortable half an hour juggling with food, fighting off spaghetti invasions, as Tommy drove around town like a madman (the only way he knew how to drive), doing handbrake turns whenever we were on the wrong road. When we got back to the track, we served up the resulting mess; a cold mixture of pizza and pasta, but I seem to remember that this was welcomed by Eddie and the boys in the pit garage – after a suitable amount of abuse for having taken so long.

JOE SAWARD Journalist

OLIVIER BERETTA

SPAGHETTI BOLOGNESE

Reigning FIA GT2 Champion, Chrysler Viper GTS-R
1998 GT2 Champion, ORECA team, Chrysler Viper

Hardwick/Sutton

Heat 2 tbsp olive oil in a saucepan.

Add the minced beef or lamb, onion and celery and cook, stirring continuously for about 5 minutes or until the meat is browned.

Add the flour, garlic and tomato purée and cook, stirring for about 1 minute.

Pour in the stock and wine then add the tinned tomatoes, salt, pepper and oregano. Bring to the boil.

Cook, stirring, until the mixture has thickened.

Lower the heat and simmer very gently, stirring occasionally for about 1 hour.

Cook the spaghetti in boiling, salted water for 8-10 minutes or until just tender, then drain thoroughly. Return the spaghetti to the saucepan and add the remaining olive oil and toss gently to coat.

Divide the pasta between plates and ladle some sauce on top.

Sprinkle generously with Parmesan cheese.

---

3 tbsp olive oil
1lb /500g ground beef or lamb
1 large onion, finely chopped
2 celery stalks, sliced
1 tbsp plain flour
2 cloves garlic, crushed
3oz/ 90g tomato purée
$\frac{1}{4}$ pint / 150 ml beef stock
$\frac{1}{4}$ pint / 150 ml red wine
13oz / 1 x 400g can chopped tomatoes
fresh ground salt and black pepper
oregano to taste
1 lb / 500 g spaghetti
fresh grated Parmesan cheese

Sutton

ENRIQUE BERNOLDI

PASTA PESTO

1998 Formula 3 Driver: 2nd British Formula 3 Championship, Promatecme UK
1999 Formula 3000 Driver: Sauber Junior Team

Serves 4 to 6
1lb any fresh pasta
36 basil leaves
3 cloves of garlic
5oz /150g pine nuts
4oz/ 100g freshly grated mixed
Pecorino Romano and Parmesan
cheese
7 fl oz / 200ml good olive oil
salt and freshly ground black pepper

This dish could be made with ready prepared pesto sauce but will taste even better with this easy fresh basil sauce.

Wipe the basil leaves with a damp cloth. Place the clean, dry leaves in a food processor together with the garlic.

Turn on the machine and gradually add the nuts and then the cheese and olive oil.

Add salt and pepper.

Cook the pasta, but avoid over-cooking.

The pesto sauce is never cooked but 2 or 3 tablespoons of pasta water should be added before the sauce is stirred thoroughly into the drained pasta. Make sure that every strand of pasta is coated with the sauce.

The pesto sauce can be made in advance and frozen.

RICARDO ROSSET

BUCATINI CON SALSA DI CARNE E PEPERONI ROSSO
Bucatini with Meat and Red Pepper Sauce

1995 2nd Formula 3000 Championship
1996-1998 Formula 1 Driver: Arrows, Lola, Tyrrell

Sutton

Heat some oil in a heavy pan, cook the onion and garlic (crushed) until golden, add the mince and cook until brown.

Add the chopped tomatoes, sliced red peppers and chopped parsley.

Lower the heat and cook for a few minutes.

Add the stock and seasoning and simmer for 30 minutes.

Cook the pasta in boiling salted water until 'al dente' (soft but still with some bite).

Drain and mix with 2 oz Parmesan cheese, place in a large dish and pour over the sauce.

Serve with more Parmesan on the side, a green salad and crusty bread.

8oz (225g) best minced beef
3 large tomatoes, peeled
1 onion, chopped
2 red peppers, de-seeded and sliced
2 cloves of garlic
olive oil
salt and freshly ground black pepper
fresh parsley
1/4 pint/150ml meat stock
fresh grated Parmesan cheese
12oz (350g) Bucatini or similar pasta

Sutton

RIGATONI AVIGNON

1998 – 1999 Formula 3 Driver Portman Arrows, Ralt
1999 MGF Driver

Warren often eats at the Paris Texas restaurant in Newcastle with his girlfriend. He always orders their Rigatoni Avignon so much so that he no longer has to ask, they just bring it for him.

1 large onion, finely chopped
4 tblsp olive oil
1 fresh green chilli, cored, de-seeded and thinly sliced
5 garlic cloves, crushed
2 ripe tomatoes, peeled, de-seeded and diced
2 tblsp chopped parsley
1/2 tsp dried oregano
salt and freshly ground black pepper
grated parmesan cheese
1lb /500g Rigatoni pasta

Remove and discard the seeds and cores from the peppers, cut in half.

Place under hot grill until skins are charred, peel and cut the flesh into thin strips.

Heat the oil in a frying pan, add the onion and fry gently until soft.

Add the peppers and chilli and cook for 2 minutes.

Stir in the garlic and cook for 1 minute.

Add the tomatoes and parsley and cook for 3 minutes or until thickened.

Remove from the heat and add the oregano and salt and pepper.

Cook the Rigatoni in a large saucepan of boiling, salted water for 8 to 10 minutes until just tender.

Drain thoroughly.

Add the sauce and toss until completely coated.

Sprinkle generously with freshly grated Parmesan cheese.

MARIO HABERFELD

Formula 3000 Driver West Competition Team
1998 British Formula 3 Champion, Stewart Racing

PEDRO LAMY

Chrysler Viper GTR Driver
1993-1995 Formula 1 Driver: Lotus, Minardi

Paul Sutton

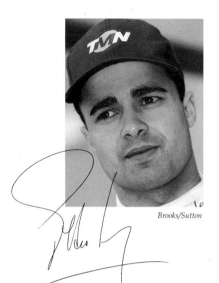

Brooks/Sutton

SPAGHETTI CARBONARA

Serves 4 to 6

1lb spaghetti (or any kind of pasta)

5 eggs

4fl oz / 100ml double cream

salt and freshly ground black pepper

1 tblsp/15ml olive oil

1oz/ 25g butter

7oz / 200g streaky bacon

4oz / 100g freshly grated Parmesan and Pecorino Romana cheese (half and half)

Beat the eggs and cream together with a pinch of salt.

Heat the oil and butter in a large pan. Add the diced bacon and cook gently until the fat becomes transparent.

Cook the spaghetti in a large pan of boiling salted water. Do not over-cook.

Drain the pasta and add it to the pan of bacon. Stir well.

Remove the pan from the heat and stir in the beaten eggs and cream and a small quantity of the cheese.

The eggs will coagulate as they come into contact with the hot pasta so it is very important to do this quickly.

Stir until each strand of pasta is coated with a thick yellow cream.

Stir in the rest of the cheese and freshly ground black pepper to taste.

Serve immediately.

1998-1999 Formula 3 Driver: Stewart Racing
1998 3rd British Formula 3 Championship, Stewart Racing

1998 Won British Formula 3 Championship, Stewart Racing
1999 Formula 3000 Driver: West Competition Team

Ryder/Sutton

Paul Sutton

BRAZILIAN BROWN BEANS
AND WHITE RICE

Both Brazilian drivers told Racey Recipes, that the following dish was what they really loved to eat.

8oz /250g red kidney beans, soaked overnight or canned ready to use

1 large Spanish onion, finely chopped

5 fl oz /150ml Beef stock (fresh if possible)

1oz / 25g butter

10ml / 2 tsp flour

1.5ml / $\frac{1}{4}$ tsp cumin powder

1.5ml / 1 tblsp chilli seasoning

1 bouquet garni, made from 2 sprigs of thyme, 1 celery stalk and 1 bay leaf

salt and freshly ground black pepper

lemon slices and flat leaved parsley to serve

white rice

Drain the beans and place them in a large saucepan.

Stir in the finely chopped onion and garlic and cover with 600ml /1 pint water.

Bring to the boil for 10 minutes then reduce the heat, cover and simmer for about 1 hour or until the beans are soft but still whole.

If tinned beans are used, this time may be reduced. Drain well.

Put the stock in a clean saucepan and bring to the boil.

In a small bowl, cream the butter and flour to a smooth paste.

Add the cumin powder and chilli seasoning and blend well.

Add the paste to the stock very gradually, stirring well until completely blended.

Add the drained beans, onion and garlic and the bouquet garni.

Season to taste with salt and freshly ground black pepper, bring to a simmer and cook covered for

45 minutes or until the sauce is smooth and rich, stirring occasionally.

Remove the bouquet garni and serve on a bed of white rice.

Garnish with lemon slices and chopped flat leaved parsley.

FAVOURITE RESTAURANTS

DERMOT BAMBRIDGE

Goodyear Formula 1 P.R.1998

CAN TRAVI NOU

Final C/, Jorge Manrique, S/N, Parc de la Vall d'Hebron, 08035, BarcelonaTel 428 19 17.

Like many in F.1, Barcelona becomes a second home during the winter with so much testing going on. Previously, my favourite restaurant was the Set Portes (I think this is Catalan for 7 Gates) by the harbour in Barcelona. One night I tried to book a table there but it was fully booked and the porter at my hotel recommended the Can Travi Nou. On first approaching it I was a bit apprehensive as it is in an area covered with tower blocks but right in the middle is this lovely walled garden surrounding a bougainvilla draped old manor house which is the restaurant. The building, the gardens and the food are superb - all in the old Catalan style – what's more their Créme Catalan is superb.

IVAN CAPELLI

" DA ORLANDO'

Cusaso, Milano.

WIN PERCY

The restaurant of the Hotel des Bains, Robertville, Nr. Spa, Belguim

Win's favourite meal here is Palma ham with melon, followed by a medium Chateaubriand steak enjoyed with a full red wine (preferably Australian) and followed by a selection of ice cream.

This is his resting place when racing at Spa, his favourite circuit after eleven 24 Hour Touring Car race starts (even winning a couple), he knows the area well.

JOHN THORNBURN

LE MOULIN GOUMAND

When we were racing at NOGARO. We went to a local restaurant in AIRE-SUR-L'ARDOUR, nothing to look at from the outside but great local cuisine, and the co-owner, a lovely lady, recommended her own foie gras. It was poached in sweet wine and apples and was sensational. Highly recommended.

AN EVENING WITH MR. E.

Journalist. The Observer/BBC Radio 5 Live

One of the good things about having Bernie Ecclestone at the dinner table is you get served first. We noticed that when he sat with us for the first three courses and then moved to another table for the remaining four. The procedure has been for five immaculate waiters to emerge, line astern from the kitchen, solemnly carrying two plates each. Circling the table, they would pause and place the food in a silent display of synchronised serving. Then they would retreat, only to repeat the process at adjoining tables.

So, Bernie moves to another table and, for the next course, the parade of food-bearing servants walks straight past us. We're left to drool for five minutes and served last: the equivalent of being transferred from Ferrari to Minardi and finding yourself at the back of the grid. Mind you, Mr E. was receiving the treatment because he was the man picking up the tab. Or, at least, we hoped he was because the rag-tag collection of media guests left the premises without contributing to what must have been a substantial total of Belgian Francs. Talk about gratitude.

As you might have gathered, this was not a Belgian Branch of the Chef and Brewer. It was one of those very smart establishments which does not sully it's doors and walls with signs. Not even when it comes to indicating which room has been set aside for 'Dames' and which has been reserved for 'Hommes'. Perhaps people who inhabit these places don't go to the loo. Or maybe they have someone to do it for them. It occurred to me, as I tiptoed with increasing desperation from one palatial room to another, that maybe I was supposed to follow that quaint Belgian habit by stepping outside, standing before all and sundry and peeing on the grass verge. After all, we were told this was an informal evening.

The mood was set by our host- no, no, nothing to do with the aforementioned - as he removed his spectacles, peered into a small dish of immaculate nouvelle cuisine, and muttered something to the effect that he hadn't noticed a big 'M' over the door as he came in. Right enough, it looked like chicken nuggets with attitude.

Despite appearances, the food was of the highest quality. Our host was surrounded by journalists but none of us would write a single word about the food or anything else. It was the sort of evening where you came away saying "very nice indeed- but what was that all about?"

cakes &

puddings

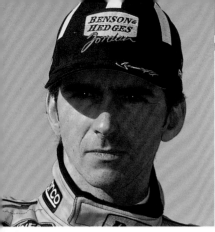

Sutton

DAMON AND GEORGIE HILL

STICKY TOFFEE PUDDING

Damon Hill OBE Formula 1 Driver: Jordan

Damon and Georgie's friends, Colin and Carol have a wonderful old house in Kent where occasionally, the entire Hill family enjoy leisurely Sunday lunches finished off with Damon's favourite, Carol's delicious Sticky Toffee Pudding.

1996 Formula 1 World Champion, Williams
1992 -1999 Formula 1 driver: Brabham, Williams, Arrows, Jordan
Grand Prix wins: 22
The first son of a Formula 1 World Champion, to win the Formula 1 World Championship.

He recentley launched his own 'wild and whacky races' television show for Channel 5.

Damon was not averse to the odd pizza, until a certain television commercial he made with Murray Walker, forced them both to eat vast quantities of the stuff. A case of too much giggling and too many retakes!

DAMON GOES BANANAS

We all know how serious racing drivers are about their boring diets. A group of us British journalists had dinner with Damon Hill in a restaurant near Hockenheim the night before the 1996 German Grand Prix. While we worked our way through the 'menu gastronomique' Damon picked at a few grains of rice and the odd lettuce leaf but when the dessert trolley arrived he crumbled, and helped himself to a banana split. With me admonishing him, he spooned away this hefty pud with enthusiasm and next day he scored a magnificent victory, going on to clinch that year's World Championship title. Even for Formula 1 drivers, a little of what you fancy does you good..

Simon Taylor
Chairman, Haymarket Magazines Ltd.

6oz stoned dates (chopped packet rolled in sugar are good and easy)
6oz granulated sugar
2oz butter
8oz self raising flour
1 large egg
$\frac{1}{2}$ tsp bicarbonate of soda
1 tsp vanilla essence

SAUCE
$2\frac{1}{2}$oz soft dark brown sugar
$1\frac{1}{2}$oz butter
2 tblsp double cream
(I use double these quantities)
Melt together stirring on a lowish heat until melted and blended

You will need a well buttered tin, approx. 11"x7"x1$\frac{1}{2}$" Make the pud first, then the sauce whilst the pud is baking.

Soak the dates in $\frac{1}{2}$ pint of boiling water for at least 20 minutes.

Cream the butter and granulated sugar thoroughly then beat the egg into the mixture.

Stir in the flour (sifted) with a fork. Add the vanilla to the drained, soaked dates. Just before adding the sloppy mixture to the flour/sugar/butter one, add the bicarbonate of soda to the dates and stir well.

Tip the sloppy lot into the floury lot and fork, mix well to form a battery textured mixture which you then tip into the well buttered tin and bake in a pre-heated oven 350F/180C for 35 minutes.

As soon as the pud comes out of the oven, pour all the sauce (if using single quantities) or half (if using double) over the pud. Serve hot or allow to cool.

If you want to re-heat the pudding. The heat from a turned off oven (when you've taken the roast out, say) is quite enough.

APPLE STRUDEL AND SOUR CHERRY STRUDEL

Bernie Ecclestone, Chief Executive Officer, Formula One Administration Ltd
Vice-President, Fédération Internationale de l'Automobile, Promotional Affairs

Sporting Pictures (UK)

Bernie Ecclestone, the Tzar of Grand Prix motor racing, began his racing career as a motor-cycle rider and successful driver (Cooper, Connaught); then as team owner of Brabham which won two world championships. He sold the team to concentrate on business and moved into administration and promotion of the sport representing all the Formula 1 teams. A visionary with legendary negotiating skills, Bernie has developed Grand Prix racing and the FIA Formula 1 World Championship into one of the world's greatest sporting spectacles, watched by a global audience, thanks to television, that can be counted in billions.

Sieve flour into a warm bowl, make a well in the centre and stir in the vegetable oil. Mix in 4 dessertspoons warm water as required to form a soft dough.

Knead the dough, turn it out on to a floured board and roll into a long sausage shape.

Pick up by one end and hit it against the pastry board.

Repeat this lifting and hitting process, picking it up by alternate ends for about 10 minutes.

Or until bubbles appear under the surface.

Knead the dough into a ball and leave to rest on a plate under an inverted warm bowl for 30 minutes.

Spread a large clean tea towel and sprinkle with flour.

Roll out the dough on the cloth into a long rectangle as thinly as possible.

Brush with warm oil to keep it pliable.

Put your hands under the dough and stretch it over the backs of your hands until the dough is paper thin. Work on one area at a time. The dough should be nearly transparent.

Trim the edges.

APPLE STRUDEL

Peel the apples and grate them.

Fry the breadcrumbs in butter.

Spread over the drawn dough.

Sprinkle grated apple, sultanas or raisins, sugar, vanilla sugar, cinnamon and rum.

Spread the filling evenly over the dough.

SOUR CHERRY STRUDEL

Fry the breadcrumbs in butter.

Spread over the drawn dough.

Arrange stoned sour cherries on top.

Sprinkle with sugar, vanilla sugar and cinnamon.

Roll up with the help of a cloth and place on a greased tin. Brush with melted butter and bake for 40 minutes 200C/400F/Gas mark 6. Sprinkle with sugar while still hot.

APPLE STRUDEL and SOUR CHERRY STRUDEL
4oz (120g) plain flour
4 dstsp vegetable oil
2oz (60g) unsalted butter
flour for rolling
oil for brushing

APPLE STRUDEL
3lbs (1½ kg) cooking apples
4oz (120g) sugar
2¾ oz (80g) butter
2½ oz (60g) breadcrumbs
2oz (50g) sultanas or raisins
vanilla sugar
caster sugar for sprinkling
cinnamon and rum
OR
SOUR CHERRY STRUDEL
2oz (50g) butter
1½ lbs (700g) sour cherries, stoned
2½ oz (60g) breadcrumbs
5oz (150g) sugar
cinnamon
vanilla sugar
caster sugar for sprinkling
butter for brushing

ROZATA

Bernie Ecclestone, Chief Executive Officer, Formula One Administration Ltd
Vice-President, Fédération Internationale de l'Automobile, Promotional Affairs

*Dubrovnik inhabitants think that their rozata is something
completely different. In the past, cooks would use rose oil drops, as
flavouring. This recipe is served all the way up the Adriatic coast
with many regional variations.*

Sporting Pictures (UK)

Sporting Pictures (UK)

1³/₄ pints (1 litre) milk
11oz (300g) granulated sugar
7 eggs
2 egg yolks
4oz (100g) granulated
sugar for caramel
butter to coat moulds
a little lemon rind

Put the milk, sugar, vanilla sugar and lemon rind to
cook in a saucepan. Cool.

Beat the eggs and the egg yolks, mix with the milk.

To make the caramel: put the sugar in a saucepan
with a little water and allow to caramelize until
golden brown.

Butter a large mould or several individual moulds
and coat with the caramel.

Pour in the milk mixture.

Place in oven 220C/425F/Gas mark 7 for 40 minutes
(for a large mould) or 20 minutes (for smaller
moulds). When half cooked, place in a bain-marie and
continue to bake.

It is also possible to cook them, covered in a steamer.

1989 British Formula Ford 1600 Champion
McLaren Autosport BRDC Winner
1994-1999 Formula 1 Driver: Williams, McLaren
Grand Prix wins: 4

DAVID COULTHARD

PIT STOP SOUFFLE

Formula 1 Driver: McLaren

Sporting Pictures (UK)

*This is the winning recipe on Celebrity Ready,
Steady, Cook - Chef, Paul Rankin.
BBC1 Television. Jan 21st 1998*

Preheat oven 190C/375F/Gas mark 5

Grease 2 ramekin dishes with butter.

Cut a thick slice off the top of the orange and using a teaspoon, remove the flesh from the inside of the orange.

Melt the butter in a pan, add the flour and mix to make a roux. Cook gently for 2 minutes and gradually add the milk. Bring to the boil, stirring to thicken the sauce. Allow to cool slightly and mix in the egg yolks and zest.

Whisk the egg whites until they form soft peaks and fold into the sauce with the caster sugar. Pour in to the hollow orange and ramekin dishes.

Bake for about 12-15 minutes or until well risen and golden. Serve.

1 orange and grated zest of 1 orange
15g/½ oz butter
plus extra for greasing
15g/½ oz plain flour
150ml/¼ pint milk
2 eggs, separated
1 tblsp caster suger

Sporting Pictures (UK)

Mobil ❶ Feel the difference

Titan Group

SOUPE AUX FRUITS EXOTIQUES

Wife of the late Mike Hailwood, Nine-times Motor-cycle World Champion,
Twelve-times winner IoM TT, won Senior IoM TT (again in 1979)
Formula 1 Driver: Reg Parnell Racing, Surtees, McLaren

1 small papaya
16 lychees
20 strawberries
2 kiwi fruit
8 passion fruit
1 tblsp finely chopped mint

SYRUP
6 tblsp sugar
a sprig of mint
1 clove
$\frac{1}{4}$ tsp mixed Chinese spices
thinly sliced zest of 1 lime
thinly sliced zest of $\frac{1}{4}$ lemon
1 vanilla pod, split lengthwise
$\frac{1}{2}$ tsp finely chopped root ginger
2 coriander seeds

Light, delicious and rather more interesting than a normal fruit salad.

To make the syrup: In a thick bottomed saucepan, combine sugar, mint sprig, clove, Chinese spices, zest of lime and lemon, split vanilla pod, root ginger (finely chopped) coriander seeds and 3/4 pint of water and bring to the boil, stirring to dissolve the sugar.

Remove from heat and leave to infuse until cool.

Meanwhile, peel papaya and cut flesh into even sized pieces. Skin lychees and remove stones. Wash and hull strawberries. Peel kiwi fruits and slice thinly.

When syrup is cool, strain through a fine sieve into a bowl.

Add prepared fruits. Cut the passion fruits and spoon out seeds and juice into a bowl of syrup.

Chill for 2 or 3 hours.

To serve: Divide fruits between shallow bowls; spoon over syrup and decorate with finely chopped mint.

Chris Meek sponsors Pauline Hailwood's Racey Recipe

Bernie Ecclestone, the Tzar of Grand Prix motor racing, began his racing career as a motor-cycle rider and successful driver (Cooper, Connaught); then as team owner of Brabham which won two world championships. He sold the team to concentrate on business and moved into administration and promotion of the sport representing all the Formula 1 teams. A visionary with legendary negotiating skills, Bernie has developed Grand Prix racing and the FIA Formula 1 World Championship into one of the world's greatest sporting spectacles, watched by a global audience, thanks to television, that can be counted in billions.

BERNIE AND SLAVICA ECCLESTONE

PANCAKES WITH WALNUTS AND WINE CHAUDEAU

Bernie Ecclestone, Chief Executive Officer, Formula One Administration Ltd
Vice-President, Fédération Internationale de l'Automobile, Promotional Affairs

Sporting Pictures (UK)

Mix the egg with the egg yolk and a pinch of salt. Gradually add the flour and milk or water. Heat a small quantity of oil in a large frying pan. Pour a small amount of batter into the centre and tip the pan to form a thin pancake. Turn the pancake when the underside is brown and briefly cook the other side.

Fill the pancakes with a mixture of crushed walnuts, cinnamon and sugar.

To make the wine chaudeau: Beat the eggs yolks, eggs and sugar, add the wine and place in a bain-marie or double boiler in which the water is not quite boiling.
Whisk until the mixture becomes a thick foam.

Arrange pancakes on a hot plate and pour over the wine chaudeau.

BATTER
4½ oz (130g) flour
1 egg
1 egg yolk
12 fl oz (250ml) milk or mineral water
salt
oil

FILLING
3oz (80g) walnuts
⅔ oz (20g) sugar
cinnamon
vanilla sugar

WINE CHAUDEAU
2 egg yolks
2 eggs
4 tblsp sugar
10 fl oz (30ml) white wine

102

CHOCOLATE PECAN PIE

Paul Stewart, Managing Director, Stewart Grand Prix

Sporting Pictures (UK)

"As far as I am concerned, this can only be served hot with vanilla ice cream heaped on top. It might be worth mentioning that it is a good source of energy for qualifying!"

Oven set at 180C/350F/Gas mark 4.

Roll out the pastry and line a tart tin (preferably loose-bottomed) approx 10in or 26cms in diameter. Prick the base with a fork and put in the fridge while you prepare the filling.

Melt the chocolate, butter, cream, golden syrup and sugar in a saucepan over a gentle heat until it is completely dissolved (do not allow to boil).

Beat in the eggs and pecan nuts.

Pour into the prepared pastry case and cook in the oven for 1 hour.

This can be prepared the day before or can be frozen.

Serve it hot or cold with ice cream, fromage frais or crème frâiche.

It serves 8 and will freeze well.

9oz (250g) ready made short crust pastry
7oz (200g) dark continental chocolate
2oz (50g) butter
1/4 pint(150ml) double cream
4 tblsp golden syrup
4 tblsp soft brown sugar
7oz (200g) shelled pecan nuts
4 eggs

Paul Stewart, son of Jackie and Helen Stewart

Paul graduated from Duke University, North Carolina with a degree in Political Science. 1988 established Paul Stewart Racing. As racing driver he won in Formula Ford 2000 and Formula 2, he also contested the Formula 3000 championship and won in the GTO Class at the Daytone 24 Hours. 1994 Paul moved into management, to concentrate on PSR's track activities (PSR have won 13 championship titles to date). 1996 Paul and Jackie Stewart announced the creation of Stewart Grand Prix. 1997 2nd Monaco Grand Prix, Rubens Barrichello (their fifth Grand Prix). Like many drivers Paul likes his puddings and this one is one of his favourites.

BANANA STANDBY

Team Owner of Hesketh Racing
President, British Racing Drivers' Club (BRDC)

Lord Hesketh gave James Hunt his 'first break' in Formula 1. Two years later, James won the 1975 Dutch Grand Prix for Hesketh Racing.

Claire's very un P.C. Pudding

"The following has always gone down well when I've needed a pudding at short notice. As you can see this is not a p.c.pud but is very quick, very fattening and very popular.

Melt butter in non-stick fry pan.

Add sugar, melt.

Add cream.*

Add bananas sliced lengthways. Simmer 3-5 mins depending on ripeness.

*or, Put in serving dish in hotplate for 10 minutes.

4-6 servings

6 bananas
1oz (30gm) butter
3 tblsp brown sugar
1 carton cream, single or double

Collins/Sutton

PAUL AND PATRICIA RADISICH

PAVLOVA

6 egg whites
1/4 tsp salt
1/4 tsp cream of tartar
2 cups caster sugar
1 tblsp cornflour
1 tblsp malt vinegar
2 tsp vanilla essence
whipped cream

SUGGESTED TOPPINGS
Fresh sliced kiwi fruit, bananas
and passion fruit pulp.
Chopped chocolate walnuts
and crystallised ginger.
Strawberries, raspberries
and blackberries,
dusted with icing sugar.

In a large metal or glass bowl, whisk the egg whites, salt and cream of tartar until soft peaks form. Gradually add the caster sugar a teaspoon at a time, whisking continuously until all the sugar has been added and incorporated into the egg whites.

The mixture should be very thick, shiny and glossy.

Sift cornflour over the egg white and fold in, then fold in vinegar and vanilla.

Spoon the mixture on to a tinfoil or baking-paper-covered baking tray, smoothing out to a dinner plate sized circle.

Bake in a low oven, 140C turning down if the Pavlova starts to colour.

Bake for 1½ hours or until crisp and dry with a cracked top.

Cool on a tray then carefully peel off the paper or tinfoil when cold.

Spread the top generously with whipped cream and garnish with fruit.

Softly spoken Kiwi, Paul Radisich, captured the coveted Touring Car World Cup crown twice in 1993 and 1994. However, after several BTCC seasons with Ford and Peugeot, he's now rebuilding his tin-top career in Australia.

"Australians often try and take credit for this recipe, however it is a true NEW ZEALAND creation and I love it! I have a terrible sweet tooth - it's just lucky that I enjoy my fitness regime. I remember Patricia's mother (who is English but was trying to make me feel welcome with a Kiwi recipe) making this for me when I first met her. It was a good start to getting on with the mother-in-law!! A true Pavlova has a crusty outside and a chewy centre."

CROSTATA DI MELE (APPLE TART)

Chief Executive, Benetton Formula 1

The youngest Chief Executive of any Formula 1 team in the pit lane, twenty nine year old Rocco Benetton first joined Benetton Formula as Commercial Director in 1997. Rocco finished his education in America, gaining an Engineering Degree at Boston University; he entered the business community with the Oppenheimer bank, then Alpha Investment Management, rising from consultant to Managing Director. In just two years of his appointment the company was managing a 1.5 billion dollar capital and nearly 300 million dollars in investment venture capital.

The youngest son of Luciano Benetton, Rocco gives us a taste for his passion for Italy and food with his favourite meal.

Rocco Benetton's favourite meal is:
Insalata di Ricola
(Rocket Salad)
Pasta con Mozzarella, pomodoro e Basilico
(Pasta with Mozzarella, Tomato and Basil)
Carpaccio con formaggio Grana
(Sliced beef with Parmesan Cheese)
Crostata di Mele
(Apple Tart)
Caffe
(Coffee)

Preheat oven to 200C/400F/Gas mark 6.

Cut the fat into the flour and then rub lightly to breadcrumb texture, add the beaten egg if used and enough cold water to bind into a ball. Place in the fridge to relax.

Mix the apple with the lemon juice to stop it from going brown.

Roll out the pastry and line a flan tin. Prick the base and cover with greaseproof paper and baking beans and bake for 10 minutes, remove beans and paper and return it to the oven to dry out the base (approx another 5 minutes).

Reduce the oven heat to 160C/325F/Gas mark 3.

Add the beaten eggs, butter and sugar to the apples, pour into the cooked pastry case and bake in the oven for 20 minutes.

Allow to cool and decorate with the whipped double cream.

8oz shortcrust pastry:
For preference use Italian OO flour,
8oz flour to 4oz fat
($^1/_2$ lard $^1/_2$ butter)
1 egg if you want a richer pastry

2 apples, grated
grated rind and juice of a lemon
3 medium eggs, beaten
3 oz (90g) unsalted butter
3 oz (90g) caster sugar
4 fl oz (120ml) double cream

LE PAVE AU CHOCOLATE

BTCC Driver Ford Mondeo Team

"This is a recipe I got from my mum (I also got my sweet tooth from her.) who got it from her mum, who got it from etc. I'm not sure that I should own up to it but when I was 16 or 17, I was known to eat half a 'Pave' while watching a Formula 1 Grand Prix on television. Of course I wouldn't do it anymore... diet is too important to a racing driver. I trust that anybody who likes chocolate will love it!'

Switzerland's best racing driver since the days of Clay Regazzoni, Alain Menu has been the BTCC's most successful racer in recent years. He was champion in 1997 having been bridesmaid for the three previous seasons. Alain admits that he binges at Christmas but then prepares for each season by going on a strict New Year diet.

Serves 12
6 egg yolks
300g butter
300g sugar
300g chocolate, (200g of plain/ 100g milk chocolate). I use CAILLER (made by Nestle) which is the best chocolate there is........ Swiss, you see. But I don't think it is sold abroad.
27 sponge finger biscuits

Whisk the yolks and sugar together in a big salad bowl until you get a creamy texture.

Add the butter (which mustn't be melted) in small portions using a mixer until you get a creamy texture again.

Melt the chocolate (better use a bain marie in order not to burn it!) then add it to the yolks, sugar, butter mixture, using the mixer again until you get back to that creamy texture once more.

Get a bread loaf tin with a base measurement of roughly 10cm x 30cms, line it with kitchen foil (this has to be slightly higher than the tin) then proceed with piling some of the mixture into the tin, levelling it with a spoon,

Add 9 sponge fingers (3 x 3) on top of it.

Repeat the operation twice so that you end up with three layers of sponge finger biscuits.

Finally leave the Pave au Chocolate in the freezer for a minimum of three hours.

By the way, 'Pave' means cobblestone!

Collin/Sutton

LOUISE'S GRANNY'S BREAD AND BUTTER PUDDING

Grand Prix Pitlane Reporter, ITV

Louise Goodman.

Formula One is great for foodies – you get to feast on different dishes from around the world. I love the Churrascarias in Brazil, the seafood in Portugal and just about everything that comes out of the kitchen in Italy.

Much as I enjoy sampling international flavours on my travels, its always nice to get back home to some good English fare, and when it comes to home cooking, there's nothing beats my Granny's Bread and Butter Pudding!

Spread the butter thickly onto the bread and then cut the slices into halves.

Line the bottom of a greased ovenproof dish with bread. Sprinkle with half the sultanas and sugar.

Add another layer of bread and sprinkle with the remainder of the sultanas and most of the sugar.

Put a final layer of bread on the top.

Beat the eggs and milk together and pour into the dish covering the bread well.

Sprinkle on the remaining sugar, leave to stand for a bit so the bread absorbs some of the liquid. Finally, sprinkle on some freshly grated nutmeg, then cook at 170C/340F/Gas mark 3 for about 50 minutes or until the liquid is set and the top in nicely browned.

about 6 slices of bread (crusts removed)
2oz (60g) butter
at least 3oz (90g) sultanas
1½ oz (45g) caster sugar
2 eggs
1 pint of milk
1 tsp grated nutmeg

CREMA CATALANA

P.R. Manager, Formula 1
GOODYEAR TIRE AND RUBBER COMPANY 1998

*"My favorite dish is Crèma Catalan which is the best of créme caramel and créme brûlée with a touch of cinnamon. I discovered this during winter testing in Barcelona. * The Can Travi Nou restaurant serves a superb version.' * See favourite restaurants.*

SERVES 8
1 lemon
2 pints of milk
$\frac{1}{2}$ pint of double cream
1 cinnamon stick
8 egg yolks
6oz caster sugar
$3\frac{1}{2}$ oz plain flour
9oz granulated sugar

Peel 6 wide strips from the lemon and put them in a pan with the milk, cream and cinnamon. Gently heat to boiling then simmer for 5 minutes.

Remove from heat, cover and leave to infuse for 5 minutes.

Beat the egg yolks and caster sugar until pale and fluffy, then beat in the flour.

Strain the milk mixture gradually onto the egg mixture, stirring until smooth.

Return to the pan and cook over a low heat for 7 to 10 minutes, stirring until thickened.

Pour the custard into 8 ramekin dishes, cool then chill.

Just before serving, sprinkle two generous tablespoons of granulated sugar over each dish. Place under a hot grill to brown and caramelise the sugar and custard.

Alternatively, if you have a traditional iron carameliser, you can heat it and press it onto the sugar. This is known as a cataplana and can be heated on a hob or a barbecue.

1980 Won BMW Championship
1982 Won Grovewood Award – Most Promising Commonwealth Driver
1982 Runner Up British Formula 3 Championship (to Ayrton Senna)
1984 – 1996 Formula 1 Driver: Tyrrell, Zakspeed, Williams, Brabham, Benetton,
Ligier, McLaren, Jordan
1988 World Sports Car Champion, Won IMSA Daytona 24 Hours
1990 Won Le Mans 24 Hours, Jaguar XJR
1998-1999 Formula 1 Driver: McLaren-Mercedes twin-seater demonstration car.
1999 Sports Car Driver:Toyota GT-One, Le Mans 24 Hours

MARTIN BRUNDLE

APPLE CRUMBLE WITH CINNAMON

ITV's Grand Prix Commentator, Toyota GT-One Driver

Sutton

Martin confessed to Racey Recipes that his favourite dish was Apple Crumble made by his Mum or his wife Liz. He likes it served hot with cream and ice-cream. This is Racey Recipes version of the all time favourite Apple Crumble ...

Peel, core and slice the apples. Simmer with a little water, 3 or 4 cloves and the cinnamon until soft but not too mushy. Remove the cloves and put into heat-proof dish big enough to allow space for the crumble.

For the crumble, rub the butter and sugar together until it is like breadcrumbs, not creamy.

Add the flour and stir in. Spread on the top of the apples making sure to cover them all round the edge.

Bake in a pre-heated oven at 200C/400F/Gas mark 6 for 15 minutes or until the crumble is golden.

Serve hot with custard, ice cream, or single cream.

Serves 6-8
2lbs (1 kg) cooking apples
cloves
$\frac{1}{2}$ tsp cinnamon powder or crumbled cinnamon stick
light brown sugar to taste

CRUMBLE
6oz (180g) plain flour
4 or 5oz (120-150g) butter
3oz (90g) light brown sugar, or granulated, if you must.

AL'S STRAWBERRY DIP

MILOCA

IndyCar Champion Driver
Won 4 Indy 500 titles
Three times National Champion
1978 Only Driver to win Indy Car "Triple Crown" : 500 mile races -
Indianapolis, Poconno and Ontario

Formula 1 Driver: Sauber
1995-1999 Formula 1 Driver: Forti, Ligier, Arrows, Sauber

One of only three drivers to win Championship races on paved ovals, dirt ovals and a road course in a single season. In 1985 Al Unser beat his son (Al Unser Jnr) to the National Championship by one point (Team Penske).

Misty Bustle, Al's lady, says that Al loves strawberries with this dip.

Sutton

The quietly spoken young Brazilian with a million-dollar smile, has proved that he's no push-over when it comes to Grand Prix racing. Often matching times with his illustrious team-mates, Pedro even outqualified world champion, Damon Hill on occasion. He favours light desserts and Miloca must take pole position for preparation and calories!

Miloca is a Brazilian dessert recipe that Pedro likes.

AL'S STRAWBERRY DIP
8 oz marshmallow cream
8 oz Philadelphia cream cheese
strawberries

Whip the marshmallow cream and cream cheese together, pile it onto a plate and surround it with strawberries. Pretty easy!

MILOCA
Serves 6
12 oranges
2 packs (100g each) of coconut flakes (wet and sweetened)

How to prepare:
Cut the oranges in small pieces and put them into a bowl. Then add the coconut flakes and mix everything with a spoon. If the oranges are not as sweet as you like, you can add a little bit of sugar.
The name 'Miloca' may change according to the different regions of the country.

SUGAR PIE

Formula 1 Driver: BAR

Sporting Pictures (UK)

1993 *North American Formula Atlantic Champion*
1994 *'Rookie of the Year' Champ Car,*
Forsythe-Green Team
1995 **Champ Car Champion, Team Green;*
Won Indy 500
1997 *Formula 1 World Champion, Williams*
*The youngest driver to become Champ Car
Champion.

When asked he did not hesitate to nominate Sugar
Pie as his favourite recipe. It's a typical Canadian
recipe and according to Jacques his mother makes the
best Sugar Pie in the world! It reminds him of his
childhood, of the cold winter in Quebec when he used
to eat this heavy but delicious pie.

In a bowl, mix the flour, salt and baking powder.

Cut the butter into the flour mixture using two knives or pastry fork.

Add water, a little at a time until the dough is easy to manipulate.

Divide the dough into two, roll out onto a floured surface, big enough to fit a 9 inch pie pan.

FILLING

In a medium saucepan, combine the brown sugar and flour.

Mix in the cream.

Cook over low heat stirring constantly until thick, smooth and creamy.

Remove from heat and pour into unbaked pie crust.

Cover with the second pie crust and prick it with a fork to let the steam out.

Bake in a pre-heated oven at 450/230C for 10 minutes.

Reduce heat to 350F/180C and bake for 20-25 minutes more.

Remove from the oven and let it cool down until warm.

Serve with a scoop of vanilla ice cream.

AND ENJOY IT !

PIE CRUST
$1\frac{1}{2}$ **cups of flour**
$\frac{1}{2}$ **tsp of salt**
$\frac{1}{2}$ **tsp baking powder**
$\frac{1}{2}$ **cup unsalted butter**
$\frac{1}{3}$ **cup of iced cold water**

FILLING
$1\frac{3}{4}$ **cups of brown sugar**
2 tblsp of flour
$1\frac{1}{2}$ **cups of cream**

WARM UPSIDE-DOWN PRUNE AND APPLE CAKE WITH ARMAGNAC ICE CREAM

Race Consultant
Masterchef finalist

This recipe requires some forward planning.
The syrup should be made
3 MONTHS in advance!

As a team manager for nearly four decades, John Thornburn worked with several talented drivers in their early careers, who went on to become World Champions: Denny Hulme, Jack Brabham, Keke Rosberg and Nigel Mansell. His major success came with Alan McKechnie's Formula 5000 team, winning the 1974 European Championship with British driver, Bob Evans.

Today, he manages Alex Portman in GTs and the team's Le Mans entry, also Rob Austin in Renault Sports. John's penchant and talent for cooking stems from his early years whilst travelling extensively in France with different teams; a talent he demonstrated on BBC's Masterchef.

PRUNE AND APPLE CAKE

2 Cox's apples
65g (2¹⁄₂ oz) butter
90g (3¹⁄₄ oz) caster sugar
1 vanilla pod, split
grated rind of 1 orange
70g (2¹⁄₂ oz) flour
2.5ml (¹⁄₂ tsp) baking powder
juice of ¹⁄₂ orange
40g (1¹⁄₂ oz) ground almonds
100ml (3¹⁄₂ fl oz) milk
1 egg
100g (3¹⁄₂ oz) prunes in Armagnac drained and stoned

PRUNE and ARMAGNAC ICE CREAM

200 ml (¹⁄₃ pint) milk
300ml (¹⁄₂ pint) double cream
1 vanilla pod, split
8 egg yolks
80g (3oz) sugar
200g (7oz) prunes in Armagnac, drained, stoned and chopped
75g (5 tblsp) syrup from prunes
75g (5tblsp) Armagnac

Dissolve 450g (1lb) sugar in 1 litre (1.75 pints) water, add juice of 1 orange, 2 split vanilla pods, 1 cinnamon stick and 3 tea bags. Bring to the boil and boil for 5 minutes. Discard tea bags. Add 1.5kgs (3¹⁄₂ lbs) prunes, return to boil and simmer for 3 minutes. Transfer to sterilized preserving jar. Let cool, seal and leave in a cool place for 3 days. Pour off half the syrup and top up with Armagnac. Reseal and leave in a cool place for 3 months!

PRUNE AND APPLE CAKE

Peel apples and cut each into 8 wedges, discard the core. Melt 15g (¹⁄₂ oz) butter in a pan. Add 20g (³⁄₄ oz) sugar and the apples, cook over a moderate heat for about 3 minutes until softened and beginning to caramelise.

Cream the remaining butter and sugar in a bowl until light and fluffy. Scrape the seeds from the vanilla pod and add to the mixture and stir in. Add the orange juice, ground almonds, milk and egg. Mix until smooth and creamy. Arrange the apples and prunes in greased individual 10cm (4 inch) tart tins. Spoon the cake mixture over the top and put tins on a baking sheet. Cook in a preheated oven at 200C/Gas mark 6, for 15 minutes. Invert the cakes on to individual serving plates, add a scoop of ice cream and serve at once.

PRUNE and ARMAGNAC ICE CREAM.

Put the milk, cream and vanilla pod into a heavy based pan. Bring slowly to boil over low heat. Meanwhile, whisk egg yolks and sugar in a bowl until well mixed. Pour on the hot milk, whisking all the time, then pour back in the pan. Cook over low heat, stirring continuously, till the custard is thick enough to coat the back of a spoon, DO NOT LET BOIL. Strain through a fine sieve into a bowl and add the syrup from the prunes. Transfer to ice cream machine and churn for a few minutes. Add the prunes and the Armagnac, churn until firm.

BETTE'S FAVOURITE FRUIT FLAN

Wife of the late Graham Hill OBE., (Triple Crown Winner - Formula 1 World Champion 1962, 1968; Indianapolis 500 and Le Mans 24 Hours Winner) Mother of Damon Hill OBE., (Formula 1 World Champion 1996) President, The Doghouse Owners' Club

Lynton Money

To make the flan:

Preheat oven 350F/180C/Gas mark 4.

Grease and line the base of a 9" (23cm) cake tin.

Whisk eggs and sugar over a pan of hot water until creamy.

Remove from heat and beat until cool.

With a metal spoon, fold in the flour, then the melted butter and almonds.

Pour into cake tin and cook for 30 mins or until risen and starting to shrink from sides of tin.

Turn out onto wire rack to cool. Sprinkle on liqueur if you are using it.

Arrange the fruit on the top of the flan.

Put the jam and a little cold water in a saucepan, heat to boil stirring all the time.

Remove any pips etc. from the liquid jam and brush over the fruit.

Allow jam to cool and set before serving with cream or crème frâiche.

Serves 6/8
Ingredients for flan:
3 eggs
3oz (75g) caster sugar
2oz (50g) plain flour
1$\frac{1}{2}$ oz (40g) melted butter
1oz (25g) ground almonds

Topping
A little almond liqueur, optional.
Strawberries, halved approx. 10.
Blueberries
Seedless grapes, halved
Small can of drained mandarin oranges
3 tblsp apricot jam

CHOCOLATE-CARAMEL PECAN CHEESECAKE

Don Naman, Executive Director, The International Motor Sports Hall of Fame, Talladega, Alabama, U.S.A.

2 x 8oz packets cream cheese
1/2 cup sugar
1/2 tsp vanilla
2 eggs
20 Kraft Caramels
2 tblsp milk
1/2 cup chopped pecans
1 ready to use Graham Cracker pie crust
3/4 cup semi-sweet chocolate chips

Mix cream cheese, sugar and vanilla with electric mixer on medium until well blended.

Add eggs, mix just until blended.

Melt caramels with milk in saucepan over low heat, stirring until smooth.

Spread caramel mix on bottom of pie crust, sprinkle pecans over caramel.

Pour cheese cake batter over this.

Bake at 350F/180C/Gas mark 4 for 40 minutes or until centre is almost set.

Cool and refrigerate overnight.

Just before serving place chips in a heavy duty zipper style plastic bag, place flat in microwave oven with chips in a single layer. Microwave on high for 2 – 4 minutes, massaging the bag every minute until all chips are melted. DO NOT OVERCOOK.

Cut a very small corner off the bottom of bag and drizzle melted chocolate on cheesecake.

CREAM CHEESE BROWNIES

Makes about 20 brownies
1 pkt (4oz) Baker's German Sweet Chocolate
5 tblsp light margarine
1 pkt (3oz) no fat cream cheese
1 cup sugar
3 eggs
1/2 cup plus 1 tblsp unsifted flour
1 1/2 tsp vanilla
1/2 tsp Calumet baking powder
1/4 tsp salt
1/2 cup coarsely chopped nuts
1/4 tsp almond extract

Melt the chocolate and 3 tblsp of margarine over a very low heat stirring constantly.
Cool.
Cream remaining margarine with cream cheese until softened.
Gradually add 1/4 cup sugar, creaming until light and fluffy.
Blend in 1 egg, 1 tblsp flour and 1/2 tsp vanilla.
Set aside.
Beat remaining eggs until thick and light in colour.
Gradually add remaining 3/4 cup of sugar, beating until thickened.
Add baking powder, salt and remaining 1/2 cup flour.
Blend in cooled chocolate mixture, nuts, almond extract and remaining 1 tsp vanilla.
Measure 1 cup of chocolate batter and set aside.
Spread remaining chocolate batter in a greased 9 inch square pan.
Top with cheese mixture.
Drop measured chocolate batter from a tablespoon on to this mixture, swirl with spatula to marble.
Bake at 350F for 35 to 40 minutes. Cool then cut into squares, cover and store in the refrigerator.

INTERNATIONAL
MOTOR SPORTS
HALL OF FAME   Talladega, Alabama
OFFICIAL SPONSOR

CREME BRULEE

BBC Broadcaster and Commentator

When Murray Walker quit the BBC, former British Touring Car Championship racer Charlie Cox stepped into the breech. The Aussie turbo-talker certainly has the gift of the gab – Charlie's acerbic touring car commentaries are some of the highlights on BBC Grandstand.

Oven 350F/180C/Gas mark 4

Mix the egg yolks and sugar together in a bowl until they go pale in colour.

Slowly bring the cream to the boil, then pour the cream into the egg and sugar mixture.

Whisk for a minute then sit the bowl over a pan of hot water and stir all the time until the custard thickens.

Divide the custard into 6 ramekin dishes, put them in a roasting tray and pour hot water into the tray to ³/₄ of the way up the sides of the dishes. Finish cooking in a pre-heated oven for 25 minutes (middle shelf).

Tip: Allow enough room around each dish for the water to be evenly distributed.

Allow to cool thoroughly before storing in the fridge. Creme brûlée tastes better at room temperature so only put it in the fridge if you decide to cook it the day before.

To make the topping:

Put the nuts and sugar in a saucepan and cook slowly stirring all the time until the sugar is a golden colour. Then just pour onto a tray which has been oiled, spread the toffee mixture out quickly and leave to set. Break the praline into pieces and decorate the brûlées just before serving.

If you prefer, leave out the nuts and just use the sugar for the toffee topping.

8 egg yolks
2oz caster sugar
1 pint double cream
2 drops vanilla extract

PRALINE TOPPING
6oz chopped nuts
6oz caster sugar

JUDY GANLEY

LOUISIANA PECAN PIE

Raced as Judy Kondratieff
(For her full race career see her Chicken piri piri recipe)

8 fl oz light corn syrup, maple syrup or golden syrup
8oz caster sugar
4oz butter
3 eggs, well beaten
1 tsp vanilla
8oz pecan nuts
2 unbaked 9inch piecrusts

Pre heat oven to 375F/Gas mark 6

Place first three ingredients in a pan and melt over low heat making sure all sugar is dissolved. Pour the mixture into the beaten eggs stirring continuously.
Add the vanilla and the pecan nuts and mix well.

Divide equally between the two piecrusts and bake in oven for 45 minutes.
Cook until firm or until a toothpick inserted in the middle comes out clean.
Remove from oven and let cool slightly.

Serve warm with vanilla ice cream or cream.
Just as good cold and just as fattening!

CAROL HUTTON

SUMMER BRULEE

Chairman, The Doghouse Owners'Club

1 10oz carton double cream
1 500g carton natural yoghurt
a small punnet of strawberries or raspberries (or you can use frozen)
4oz (120g) brown demerara sugar

Put strawberries or raspberries in a bowl with the yoghurt and mash together.

In another bowl, whisk the cream until thick, then fold into the yoghurt/fruit mixture.

Divide between six individual ramekins, spoon brown sugar over the top to cover completely.
Place in the fridge for a couple of hours and the sugar will have caramelised, looking as though it has been under the grill.

PAT McLAREN BRICKETT

PAVLOVA -
a favourite Australasian dessert which is scrumptious, a dessert not to be missed.

Pat McLaren Brickett, Vice-President, The Doghouse Owner's Club

Lynton Money

*Wife of the late BRUCE McLAREN
(Driver and Constructor)*

Within months of establishing Bruce McLaren Racing, their first Championship series was clinched in New Zealand and Australia. In sportscars, they dominated the CanAm series, Bruce and his close friend Denny Hulme winning five consecutive titles. In Formula 1, Bruce won his first Grand Prix (1959 US GP) when just 22, making him the youngest ever winner; in 1966 he won Le Mans and debuted his McLaren M2B at Monaco (1966) and won his first Grand Prix in a McLaren M7A two years later at Spa. McLaren successes were also won in Formula 2, Formula 5000 and IndyCars. Bruce McLaren established a highly successful and professional team with a reputation for technical excellence, a reputation which is echoed in the mighty McLaren International team of today.

Heat oven to 250F/125C

Beat egg whites and salt until quite stiff.

Fold in sugar, add vanilla and vinegar.

Place on greased paper on greased tray and bake very slowly for about 1 to 1$\frac{1}{2}$ hours.

When cold, pile on whipped cream and decorate with kiwi fruit or any fruit of your choice.

**3 eggs whites
9oz (120g) caster sugar
1 tsp vinegar
1 tsp essence of vanilla
pinch of salt
whipped cream
fruit of choice**

GEORGIE SHAW

LETHAL CHOCOLATE THINGY....

This is seriously rich and not for the faint-hearted. The base is an easy all-in-one method.

Place all ingredients in food processor. Mix on high speed 12/15secs until mixed.

Pour mixture onto greased baking tray, level before baking for approx. 25 mins.

Cake should spring back when touched in the middle.

Turn out onto a wired rack to cool. Meanwhile prepare the fillings.

Cream butter in food processor for approx. 10secs on high speed. Gradually add the sifted icing sugar and cocoa. Mix thoroughly for about 15/20secs.

Transfer butter cream into a large saucepan, cook over low heat for 3/4 minutes. Add milk slowly, stirring continuously. Finally, stir for a few minutes until the mixture becomes smooth and shiny.

Remove fudge icing from heat, cover and reserve.

Whip double cream until stiff, cover and chill until required.

Assembly:

trim edges of cake and divide into three equal strips lengthways.

Sprinkle some of the rum over one of the strips, then with a palette knife gently smooth over a layer of warm fudge icing onto the cake. Repeat this process with remaining strips.

Transfer one of the strips onto a serving dish and when the icing is completely cool add a layer of the whipped cream.

Place the second strip on top of the layer of cream and repeat the process until the final strip which should be placed on top, fudge icing face down!

Cover the entire creation with a thin layer of whipped cream and decorate with the hulled strawberries and swirls of fudge icing or whipped cream along the top.

Chill for 2 hours before serving.

Serves 8/10
6oz (175g) self raising flour
2oz (60g) cocoa
8oz (225g) unsalted butter
8oz (225g) caster sugar
4 medium eggs
1 tbsp cold water
50ml dark rum
(reserve for assembly stage)
Pre-heat oven to 375F/190C/Gas mark 5. Grease a 12x16ins tin, line with greaseproof paper and lightly grease the paper.

Filling
1$\frac{1}{2}$pt (80 cl) double cream
2 drops of vanilla essence
strawberries (for decoration)

Chocolate Fudge Icing
10oz (285g) icing sugar
2oz (60g) cocoa
6oz (175g) unsalted butter
10ml milk

Working in an office can have its compensations especially when the office is the nerve-centre of a Formula 1 magazine and the perks can be the occasional team launches or Grands Prix to attend. On one such visit to Imola, on the eve' of the Grand Prix, the Editor Derek Wright, journalist Eric Silbermann and I had booked a table at a renowned hotel for dinner; the hotel favoured by Frank Williams, Ron Dennis and Ayrton Senna.

A last minute glitch whilst filing an article almost jeopardised the entire evening and meant we had little time to make the twenty mile drive from the track to our hotel to have a 'splash and dash' shower and change of clothes before leaving again. We must have set a blistering time in that 'final sector' as we had time for an aperitif in the bar. Although minutes earlier we had to side-step out of the way as a car roared past us ablaze in a mass of camera flash-lights. Ayrton and friends were obviously dining out on this occasion.

At last we arrived in the dining room where Ron Dennis and some business colleagues were already eating; I ordered pasta which was made with fresh asparagus and was quite the most delicious I have tasted. If Racey Recipes had not already been pasta'd-out I would have wished to include that recipe.

However, the Lethal Chocolate Thingy has been enjoyed by several friends including Pat McLaren Brickett whom I accompanied to the 1998 French Grand Prix. Pat had been invited as a VIP guest of McLaren International and kindly asked me to join her. It was a super trip; our accommodation was a delightful hotel, where the rooms were individual terraced cottages set in a country garden with swimming pool and beautiful al fresco restaurant - acclaimed for its food and fine wines, the local Pouilly Fumé Rose was divine. We ate breakfast in the McLaren motorhome in the Formula One paddock where Ron Dennis and Mika Hakkinen greeted us. Then when qualifying was about to begin we were escorted to the elegant surroundings of the Formula One Paddock Club and McLaren's hospitality suite, situated high above and directly over the McLaren pits. The view was superb and we were again wined and dined in style; the buffet presented each day offered a selection of lobsters, freshly grilled tiger prawns, grilled lamb, fillet steak, vegetarian pasta dishes, roasted vegetables and salads, with the lightest fruit desserts to finish. This is Grand Prix racing in style and worth experiencing at least once in a lifetime.

TARTE AU CITRON

Race Consultant
Masterchef finalist

As a team manager for nearly four decades, John Thornburn worked with several talented drivers in their early careers, who went on to become World Champions: Denny Hulme, Jack Brabham, Keke Rosberg and Nigel Mansell. His major success came with Alan McKechnie's Formula 5000 team, winning the 1974 European Championship with British driver, Bob Evans.

Today, he manages Alex Portman in GTs and the team's Le Mans entry, also Rob Austin in Renault Sports. John's penchant and talent for cooking stems from his early years whilst travelling extensively in France with different teams; a talent he demonstrated on BBC's Masterchef.

Make the pastry and chill for 30 minutes. Roll out on floured surface and line a flan tin (11 inch).

Bake blind in oven pre-heated to 200C/Gas mark 6 for 10 minutes.

Remove the baking beans and foil and bake pastry shell for 5 minutes until it has dried out.

Remove from oven and reduce temp to 180C/Gas mark 4.

Beat the eggs in a bowl and add the cream, lemon zest and sugar.

Stir until smooth and pour into the pastry shell.

Bake for 35 - 40 minutes until the filling has set. Leave to cool and dust with icing sugar.

Decorate with the lemon twists and serve warm.

9 eggs
300ml (1/2 pint) double cream
grated zest and juice of 5 big lemons
375g (12oz) caster sugar
icing sugar
lemon twists for decoration

PASTRY
250g (8oz) plain flour
125g (4oz) chilled butter, cut into cubes
60g (2oz) caster sugar
1 egg

SLICKS a.k.a Paris-Brest au Café

Originally made at our family bakery Sterrett's of Monmouth, where the recipe called for quarts of eggs, making 500+ eclairs!

This recipe will make a pair of 8 inch Slicks.

Choux pastry
2oz (60g) lightly salted butter
7½ fl oz water
pinch of caster sugar
pinch of salt
4oz (100g) flour
3 medium eggs

Filling
1½ pt/30 fl. oz double cream
2 level tblsp icing sugar
1 tsp of vanilla essence

Topping
4oz (110g) icing sugar
25ml water
2 tsp pure camp coffee essence
2oz (60g) slithered almonds (toasted)

Pre-heat the oven to 220C/425F/Gas mark 7.

Line baking tin with greaseproof paper and mark out two 20cm/8inch circles.

Put water, butter, sugar into heavy-based saucepan and bring to boil.

Remove from heat and stir in flour. Return pan to heat (low) and stir until mixture leaves sides of pan. Cook for a further one minute.

Allow mixture to cool slightly before adding eggs.

Transfer mixture to food processor, add one egg and mix (high speed) 10/12secs or until just mixed. Scrape sides of bowl and repeat process with remaining eggs.

Transfer choux pastry to piping bag and pipe out the two circles.

Bake on middle shelf for 15mins with the door slightly open (prop open with wooden spoon) then reduce heat to 200C/400F/Gas mark 6 and cook 15mins close door.

Remove from oven, allow to cool then cut Paris-Brest rings in half horizontally.

Weaned on serious sportscars driven flat-out by parents and so became hopelessly hooked on motor racing. Whilst Chairman of the British Women Racing Drivers' Club enjoyed several years as saloon/sportscar racer. An ex-restaurateur and event organiser before moving into motorsport press and public relations promoting European racing team headed by Tom Walkinshaw/Win Percy (etc) and Tony Pond/Rob Arthur (WRC) with MG Metro 6R4 at Austin Rover. Currently working as the communications manager at F1 NEWS magazine and one of the Racey Recipes collaborators.

Prepare fillings: whip cream to peak stage and fold in vanilla and icing sugar. Cover and chill until required.

Add coffee essence to icing sugar and gradually add enough water to spread with a palette knife.

Spread the coffee icing over the tops of the rings and sprinkle with toasted slithered almonds. Pipe cream onto base rings and place iced rings on top.

Slicks maybe banned for F1 but not here!

BANOFFI PIE

MGF Driver

Piers's mum Jean is one of the Racey Recipe collaborators, she works for the Red Cross as a beauty advisor specialising in cosmetic camoflage. His father, Mel raced minis and rallied in a Lotus Cortina and now runs Meltune and prepares Piers's car.

Crumb the biscuits (place in a plastic bag and crush with rolling pin).

Melt the butter in a pan and stir in crumbs.

Press the mixture over the base and sides of an 8inch round flan dish. Chill.

Put the butter and sugar in a pan, heat gently, stirring until the butter has melted.

Stir in the condensed milk, bring to the boil.

Simmer for 5 minutes stirring until it looks like caramel.

Line the crumb base with sliced bananas and pour on the caramel mixture.

Leave to set.

Slice more bananas and toss in the lemon juice.

Whip the cream and spread on the top.

Decorate with bananas and chocolate flakes.

I prefer it the way Mum does it by boiling the can, but some people do not like to do this. Mum boils the condensed milk can (unopened) in a saucepan of boiling water for two hours. Be careful not to let the saucepan go dry. Keep a kettle boiling nearby to top up the water. If you cook the condensed milk this way you will not need the butter or sugar.

CRUMB CASE
250g/8oz digestive biscuits
125g/4oz butter

FILLING
175g/6oz butter
175g/6oz caster sugar
1x425g/14oz can condensed milk
2 bananas
1 tablespoon lemon juice
150ml / ¼ pint whipping cream
1 chocolate flake

GO FASTER PRUNE AND APPLE SAUCE CAKE

Television Celebrity and GT enthusiast

225g (8oz) plain flour
225g (8oz) caster sugar
5 ml (1 tsp) baking powder
5 ml (1 tsp) ground cinnamon
2.5ml (½ tsp) ground nutmeg
1 heaped tsp cocoa powder
100g (4oz) apple sauce
250g (9oz) California stoned
prunes, chopped
175g (6oz) California raisins
100g (4oz) shelled walnuts, chopped
50g (2oz) melted butter
2 eggs, beaten

To decorate: prunes, glacé fruit
and walnuts.

Sift all the dry ingredients together into a bowl.

Add the apple sauce, prunes, raisins, nuts, butter and eggs. Beat well.

Pour mixture into a greased and lined 15-18cm (6-7inch) round tin.

Bake in a pre-heated oven at 160C/325F/Gas Mark 3 for approximately $1\frac{1}{4}$ hours or until well risen and firm. If the top becomes too brown, cover with foil.

Decorate with fruit.

DENA'S DROP DEAD DELICIOUS CAKES

We defy you to find anything more mouthwatering. Dena is my sainted cook.

Edward, my husband, is a brilliant chef - ditto Dena - so I never darken the door of the kitchen - tho' I make a mean cup of cappuccino.

Fiona Montagu.

Beat the eggs in a large bowl, gradually add the sugar to the eggs. Continue beating until thick and light. Add the vanilla.

In a separate bowl combine the flour, baking powder and salt. Stir into the egg mixture.

Bring the milk to boiling point. Add the butter to the milk. Stir into the egg mixture.

Beat well.

Pour into a greased and floured 9" (23cm) square pan.

Bake at 350F (180C) for 30 minutes.

To prepare topping, combine all the ingredients.

When cake is baked but still hot, spread with the topping mixture. Place cake under the broiler until the topping is bubbly and brown (about 4 or 5 minutes) when placed about 6" (15cm) from the broiler). WATCH CAREFULLY.

16 servings or can be cut into squares

2 eggs
1 cup (250ml) sugar
1 tsp (5ml) vanilla
1 cup (250ml) flour
1 tsp (5ml) baking powder
$\frac{1}{4}$ tsp (1ml) salt
$\frac{1}{2}$ cup (125ml) milk
1 tblsp (15ml) butter

TOPPING
1 cup (250ml) chopped nuts OR grated coconut
1/2 cup (125ml) brown sugar
1/2 cup (125ml) melted butter
1/4 cup (50ml) cream
1 tsp (5ml) vanilla

CARROT CAKE

Wife of the late Denny Hulme (Formula 1 World Champion, 1967)

"Fancy being a 'Kiwi' and living 'down under' and not being able to fly. Do you think our best asset is the long beak or the fine feathers? We certainly lay a huge egg."

"My moist carrot cake could be a dessert or a coffee break indulgence."

Lynton Money

CARROT CAKE

16oz or 3 cups of grated carrot
1 breakfast cup wholemeal flour
1 breakfast cup plain flour
1 breakfast cup vegetable oil
1½ cups raw sugar
2 tsp baking soda (level)
2 tsp cinnamon
4 medium eggs
pinch of salt

ICING

3oz cream cheese
1oz soft butter
½ tsp vanilla essence
2-3 cups icing sugar
Cream all together, spread on cake/s when cool (not cold).
Store in the refrigerator.

Mix all dry ingredients together, add the grated carrot and mix well.
Add well beaten eggs with the oil. Mix well together.
Put into 2 greased loaf tins or one square lined cake tin.
Bake ³/₄ to 1 hour at 350F

EASY CHOCOLATE SPONGE AND QUICK FRUIT CAKE

Sister, of the late Denny Hulme (Formula 1 World Champion, 1967)

EASY CHOCOLATE SPONGE

3 large eggs
½ breakfast cup cornflour
1 level tblsp golden syrup
½ tsp cream of tartar
½ breakfast cup sugar
1 tsp flour
½ tsp baking soda
1 heaped dstsp cocoa

Separate the eggs, beat whites until thick, add yolks and sugar gradually.
Add golden syrup then slowly add sifted dry ingredients.
Bake in lined sponge roll tin for 15 minutes at 375F.
When cold, cut in half and fill with whipped cream.
Ice with chocolate icing and top with nuts or sprinkle with icing sugar.

QUICK FRUIT CAKE

16oz sultanas
12oz sugar
12oz flour
1 tsp almond essence
8oz butter
3 beaten eggs
1 tsp baking powder
pinch of salt

Cover sultanas with water, boil 5 minutes, strain.
Cream butter and sugar together.
Add beaten eggs, mix in combined dry ingredients and almond essence.
Bake in lined tin for approximately half an hour at 350F.

7 time Winston Cup Champion
7 time Daytona 500 Winner
Received U.S. Medal of Freedom 1992

ANGEL FOOD CAKE

Legendary driver of NASCAR car #43
NASCAR Winston Cup all time Career Wins Leader, (200)

Sutton

Beat egg whites until foamy, add cream of tartar and beat until stiff, but not dry.

Gradually beat in sugar, add vanilla then beat in flour as gently as possible.

Bake in angel food pan at 325F/160C/Gas mark2+. For 1 hour and 15 minutes or until top is nicely browned.

1½ cups of egg whites
1 tsp cream of tartar
1½ cups of sugar
¼ tsp salt
1 cup of flour (sifted) then sift 4 times
1 tsp vanilla

Sutton

Rockingham

Britain's motorsports complex for the new millennium

126

ICE BOX COCONUT CAKE
AND RED VELVET CAKE

Don Naman, Executive Director of the International Motor Sports Hall of Fame,
Talladega, Alabama, U.S.A.

ICE BOX COCNUT CAKE

2 cups of sugar

2 cups sour cream

2 small packages frozen coconut

1 packet Duncan Hines yellow cake mix

ON THE NIGHT BEFORE

Mix together the sugar, sour cream and coconut.

Store in the refrigerator overnight.

ON THE NEXT DAY

Bake one yellow Duncan Hines cake mix according to directions on the package, divided into 2 layers.

When cool slice each layer, making 4 layers.

Spread the sugar/cream/coconut concoction from the refrigerator between the layers and on the top.

Store for 4 days in the refrigerator before serving.

RED VELVET CAKE

1 box white cake mix with pudding

3 tbs chocolate milk mix

2 bottles red food colouring

1 tsp vanilla flavouring

3 eggs

$\frac{1}{2}$ cup buttermilk

$\frac{1}{2}$ cup water

$\frac{1}{2}$ cup cooking oil

$\frac{1}{2}$ tsp vinegar

CREAM CHEESE ICING

1 box confectioners sugar

1 x 8oz pot of cream cheese

$\frac{1}{2}$ stick oleo

$\frac{1}{2}$ cup chopped pecans (optional)

(I use ready made cream cheese icing)

Mix all of the cake ingredients into a smooth batter.

Place in greased and floured round cake pans.

Bake in a pre-heated 350F/180C/Gas mark 4, oven for 25 minutes.

Cool and frost with cream cheese icing.

INTERNATIONAL
MOTOR SPORTS
HALL OF
FAME Talladega, Alabama
OFFICIAL SPONSOR

NUTTY FRUIT CAKE

Wife of the late Mike Hailwood, Nine-times Motor-cycle World Champion,
Twelve-times winner IoM TT, won Senior IoM TT (again in 1979)
Formula 1 Driver: Reg Parnell Racing, Surtees, McLaren

This is a wonderful easy 'all-in-one' method, moist, delicious cake. It is never allowed to keep for long in my house.

Prepare a cool oven. Grease a round 7" cake tin, line base with greaseproof paper and lightly grease the paper.

Peel and core the apple and cut 6 thin slices and place in a bowl of cold water.

Chop remainder. Roughly chop walnuts.

Place sugar, margarine, flour, mixed spice, eggs and milk into a mixing bowl.

Mix together with a wooden spoon, then beat for 2 or 3 minutes until mixture is smooth and glossy.

Fold in chopped apples and walnuts into the cake mixture with a metal spoon.

Place mixture in the prepared tin, levelling the top with the back of a metal spoon.

Drain the reserved apple slices and arrange in a ring around the top of the cake.

Sprinkle the top with the demerara sugar.

Bake in the centre of the oven for 1 hour 20 or 30 minutes.

Test by pressing with the fingers, if cooked the cake will spring back and will have begun to shrink a little from the sides of the tin.

Leave to cool in the tin for 15 minutes.

Turn out onto a wire rack and leave until cold.

1 large cooking apple (Granny Smith)
1oz (25g) walnuts
6oz (175g) caster sugar
6oz (175g) soft margarine
8oz (225g) self raising flour
1 rounded tsp mixed spice
3 eggs
1 tblsp milk
1oz (25g) demerara sugar

Chris Meek sponsors Pauline Hailwood's Racey Recipe

LARDY CAKE

10 oz (300g) strong bread flour
1oz (30g) lard
1/2 tsp dried yeast
a pinch of salt
a little warm milk or water

FILLING
At least 6oz (180g) mixed dried fruit
(I use more!)
6oz brown sugar
4oz (120) lard
extra lard for glazing

Mix the flour and yeast and salt, cut the lard into small cubes and mix into the flour, add the milk/water a little at a time until you have a soft dough.

Allow to rest for 5 minutes.

Knead for 5 minutes on a floured board.

Roll out into a long rectangle.

FILLING

Spread the lard in dots onto the rectangle of dough.

Spread the fruit and most of the sugar evenly onto the dough.

Fold the dough into three and seal the edges with cold water.

Glaze the dough with lard and sprinkle with sugar.

Cover with a damp cloth and put in a warm place to rise for at least 30 minutes.

Bake in a pre-heated oven 200C/400F/Gas mark 6 for 20 minutes or until the loaf is golden brown and sounds hollow when tapped underneath.

Allow to cool upside down. Pour any melted juice back over the cake.

Can be eaten cold or warm with butter.

You can put some of the fruit into the bread mix to get a more even distribution of fruit through the cake.

Who am I? An 'ex' everything! An ex-wife of an ex-racer, sister of an ex- racer/constructor/team owner, ex-film producer, ex-theatrical costumier, ex-Doghouse cabaret producer, exhausting! What I am is very grateful to my 5 fellow collaborators for their help, support and friendship in putting together RACEY RECIPES.

Lardy cake is a regional speciality of Oxfordshire although versions of it turn up in Wales, Gloucestershire and Warwickshire. It is very sweet, sticky, fattening and delicious and just the thing to keep the cold out when racing at Silverstone.

I prefer to make small cakes as the temptation to finish it off is less.

CAUTION. Seek medical assistance, this is a heart attack on a plate.

DAMON'S DELAYED PIT STOP!

Life on a plate. That's what people say about celebrity status, isn't it? Doors open, tickets materialise or reservations become miraculous vacancies. Except, that is, after a long day's testing at Silverstone. True, the table at a nearby Italian restaurant had been booked for 7pm and it was more like 8pm when we arrived, after driver briefings and engineers' meetings had eaten into the schedule. But when Damon Hill, one of Britain's most instantly familiar faces, numbers among your party and is standing right next to you, drawing the inevitable head-turning double-takes from all corners of the room, it takes some restaurant owner to show us the door. Which he did, barely batting an eyelid. "Too late. We thought you weren't coming so we let your table go to somebody else." Right. Fine. OK. If only I'd known then that the 1996 World Champion is just about word perfect on every episode of Fawlty Towers, we could have launched into a Basil-like tirade about standards.

Spanish/Italian waiters, the war and the collapse of carefully laid BBC plans for a recorded interview in a pleasantly informal setting. Damon, to his credit, was commendably untroubled by this turn of events - unlike his companion from the BBC. "We'll go to the hotel then. It's just around the corner. I'm sure they'll serve us." He was right. They did us proud. But not before another hurdle presented itself. Would the whispering couple in the corner mind if the piped music was turned off so that the BBC could make their highly sought after recording with only the sound of knives and forks as background accompaniment? Finally, some two hours behind schedule, my dinner with Damon actually took place. And by contrast, the next two flew by, without a hitch or a hiccup. The perfect guest. But I suspect he won't risk another night out on the BBC in a hurry.

by Jonathan Legard, BBC Motor Racing Correspondent

JONATHON LEGARD
BBC Motor Racing Correspondent

MOSS MISSES 107% BREW-UP QUALIFYING!

'the tea making took longer than a lap of Silverstone in reverse'

It was, as I recall, a gloomy nondescript afternoon. Typically January really. And the question when it came was entirely in keeping with the day. Mundane, utterly unremarkable.

"Can I get you a cup of tea?" Now I don't like tea. Never have. And yet there I was, blurting out quite merrily, "Oh, yes please. White, no sugar thank you." So why? Why did I say yes when I knew I'd be sipping away through gritted teeth, wishing I'd opted for the glass of water I usually request in these situations? Why? Because it's not every day you're offered a cup of tea brewed by Stirling Moss.

As Stirling set about his task, busying himself in the cupboards of his Mayfair kitchen, a BBC colleague and I sat there like two schoolchildren. We'd come to interview him for a BBC Radio series about British World Champions, and here we were being waited on by a man who in his day could have clicked his fingers and had every waitress in London vying for his order. Sitting on the sofa it was all we could do to stop ourselves recording the moment for BBC Archives. Instead we just say there mouthing at each other "Can you believe this? Stirling Moss is making us a cup of tea." As it turned out, the tea making took longer than a lap of Silverstone in reverse. Stirling couldn't find the milk. And "the office" - otherwise known as his wife, Susie - was unable to assist because she was out. Somehow from somewhere someone unearthed a longlife carton and tea was duly served.

The interview? Wonderful. Far more straightforward and much more up Stirling's street.

Nonetheless, for about the first and only time in my life the words of a good friend made sense. "You can't beat a cup of tea."

Contents

CONTENTS

CONTENTS

WEIGHTS, MEASUREMENTS AND HEAT CONVERSIONS

Because metric and imperial weights and measurements don't convert exactly or easily, don't mix them in a recipe (ie metric flour and imperial butter!) 1 ounce is actually 28 grams but is usually converted as 25 or 30. Most of the recipes translate 1 ounce as 30 grams.

Imperial	Metric	Imperial	Metric
$\frac{1}{4}$ oz	7 – 8g	1lb	450g
$\frac{1}{2}$ oz	15g	1 $\frac{1}{2}$ lb	675g
1oz	30g	2lb	900g
2oz	60g	2.205lb	1kg
4oz ($\frac{1}{4}$ lb)	110g	4lb	1.8kg
8oz ($\frac{1}{2}$lb)	225g	6lb	2.7kg
12oz ($\frac{3}{4}$lb)	340g	8lb	3.6kg

1 table spoon (tblsp) = 30g, 1 oz.
1 dessert spoon (dstsp)= 15g, $\frac{1}{2}$ oz
1 tea spoon (tsp)   = 4 g, $\frac{1}{4}$ oz

American/European	USA	Metric	Imperial
Flour, currants	1 cup	140g	5oz
Sugar, butter, margarine	1 cup	225g	8oz
Brown sugar	1 cup	170g	6oz
Sultanas, raisins, rice	1 cup	200g	7oz
Ground almonds, grated cheese	1 cup	110g	4oz
Butter	1 stick	110g	4oz
Sugar	1 level tblsp	15g	$\frac{1}{2}$ oz

Australian/European	Australian	Metric	Imperial
Fresh breadcrumbs	1 cup	55g	2oz
Desiccated coconut	1 cup	85g	3oz
Nuts (chopped) Biscuit crumbs	1 cup	110g	4oz
Flour, dry breadcrumbs	1 cup	140g	5oz
Icing sugar/brown sugar/mixed fruit	1 cup	170g	6oz
Uncooked rice	1 cup	200g	7oz
Caster sugar, butter	1 cup	225g	8oz
Honey, golden syrup, treacle	1 cup	370g	12oz

LIQUID

Imperial	Metric	Fl oz
$\frac{1}{4}$ pint (1 gill)	150ml	5
$\frac{1}{2}$ pint	290ml	10
1 pint	570 ml	20
1 $\frac{3}{4}$ pint	1 litre	35

WEIGHTS, MEASUREMENTS AND HEAT CONVERSIONS

LIQUID, AMERICAN/AUSTRALIAN/EUROPEAN

American	Australian	Metric	Imperial
½ fl oz		15ml	1 tblsp
½ cup + 2 tablespoon		150ml	¼ pint
1 ¼ cups		290ml	½ pint
1 pint, 16fl oz		5.75ml	1 pint
	1 tsp	5ml	
	1 tblsp	20ml	
	1 cup	250ml	
1 cup		225ml	8fl oz
1 egg, size 3		56ml	2 fl oz
1 egg white		28ml	1 fl oz

WINE QUANTITIES

Imperial	Metric	Fl oz.
Average wine bottle	750	25
1 glass wine	100	3
1 glass port/sherry	70	2
1 glass liqueur	45	1

LENGTHS

½ ins = 1cm,   1ins = 2.5cm,   2 ins = 5cm

6ins = 15cm,   12ins = 30cm

CENTIGRADE	FAHRENHEIT	GAS	
80	175		
100	200		
110	225	¼	
120	250	½	VERY COOL
150	300	1	COOL
180	350	4	MODERATE
200	400	6	FAIRLY HOT
220	425	7	HOT
230	450	8	VERY HOT
260	500	9	
290	550		